T0291297

Grey Behaviors after Logical Fallacies in Public and Professional Communication

This practical guide enables readers to recognize, assess, and defend against grey behaviors—attempts to persuade listeners using fallacious arguments. It provides valuable tools for communicating successfully in a wide variety of public and professional contexts.

The book examines 20 wide-ranging logical fallacies, cognitive errors, and rhetorical devices that may take place in persuasive communication, and discusses how to assess and respond the behaviour of a speaker who may be disingenuously attempting to manipulate the listener—or who may simply be mistaken. Drawing upon research and insights from communication, psychology, business management, and human resources, it considers fallacies in reasoning not just as abstract formulas, but as a feature of communication encounters such as negotiations, interviews, public debates, and personal conversations. Each form of fallacious reasoning is exemplified by dialogues in both professional settings (such as interviewing and personnel assessment) and everyday interactions in public discourse. The book then provides self-assessment tests to ensure the reader can evaluate the grey behavior in these encounters.

This book provides research-based skills and insights that will benefit students and professionals in fields ranging from communication, politics, management, human resources, organizational psychology, journalism, and anyone else looking to develop critical interaction skills.

Homayoon Kord is the Chief of Competency Assessment and Development in Mobarakeh Steel Company (MSC), Iran. He has established several assessment centers to assess and develop leadership skills, and to attract and screen talented people for expert positions. He has also developed an assessment center to identify and develop auditor talents in quality management systems (ISO and EFQM).

George C. Thornton III is Professor Emeritus at Colorado State University, USA. He received the Distinguished Alumni Award from Purdue University, the Legacy Lifetime Award from the South African Assessment Center Study Group, and the Lifetime Achievement Award from the United Kingdom Assessment Centre User Group. His most recent books include *Assessment Center Perspective for Talent Management Strategies* (2015, with Deborah E. Rupp, & Brian J. Hoffman) and *Developing Organizational Simulations: A Guide for Practitioners, Students, and Researchers* (2nd ed, 2017, with Rose A. Mueller-Hanson & Deborah E. Rupp).

Grey Behaviors after Logical Fallacies in Public and Professional Communication

Homayoon Kord and
George C. Thornton III

Routledge
Taylor & Francis Group
NEW YORK AND LONDON

First published 2021
by Routledge
605 Third Avenue, New York, NY 10158

and by Routledge
2 Park Square, Milton Park, Abingdon, Oxon, OX14 4RN

Routledge is an imprint of the Taylor & Francis Group, an informa business

Library of Congress Cataloging-in-Publication Data
Names: Kord, Homayoon, author. | Thornton, George C.,
1940– author.
Title: Grey behaviors after logical fallacies in public
and professional communication / Homayoon Kord and
George C. Thornton III.
Description: New York : Routledge, 2021. | Includes
bibliographical references and index.
Subjects: LCSH: Business communication. | Persuasion
(Rhetoric) | Fallacies (Logic) | Speech acts (Linguistics) |
Communication.
Classification: LCC HF5718 .K67 (print) |
LCC HF5718 (ebook) | DDC 658.4/5—dc23
LC record available at https://lccn.loc.gov/2021019261
LC ebook record available at https://lccn.loc.gov/2021019262

ISBN: 978-1-032-01204-9 (hbk)
ISBN: 978-1-032-01690-0 (pbk)
ISBN: 978-1-003-17961-0 (ebk)

Typeset in Times New Roman
by codeMantra

HK: my wife Fatemeh and my daughter Vania
GCT: Louise my love and friend
HK and GCT: Victims of Covid-19 and their families

Contents

Illustrations

Preface

As practitioners in assessment and development of human talent in organizations, we have often been challenged to provide accurate assessment of the veracity of claims by applicants and staff members. Naturally we are subjected to candidates' persuasive arguments. But often the speaker uses bad arguments such as logical fallacies, as well as negative rhetorical devices and social influence techniques. These may be mild expressions of misunderstanding or quite serious attempts to deceive or even lie to us. As HR specialists we need a way to make our assessment more accurate.

As citizens in interactions in everyday life, we are bombarded by attempts to mislead us. The merchant uses unfounded and exaggerated advertisements. The politician spouts bad diversionary rhetoric. The neighbor uses false reasoning. In these and many other situations, we need a way to reserve judgment, explore the speaker's intent, and accurately assess the darkness of the grey behavior.

1 Introduction

In this chapter,

- We describe the purposes of the book.
- We give background on the role of logic in persuasion.
- We help you identify types of logical fallacies.
- We show the advantages of having preventive knowledge regarding fallacious thinking.
- We show the advantages of behavioral analyses of fallacious thinking.
- We show you how to assess the level of severity of grey behaviors after a person states a logical fallacy.

We caution you that

- Communication and discussion are complex processes.
- Some logical fallacies are difficult to understand.
- Any short book cannot de-bias faulty thinkers.

⚠ **Caution!**

Communication is complex. Short dialogues may not change the speaker, listener, or reader.

Introduction

Why should you read *Grey Behaviors after Logical Fallacies in Public and Professional Communication*?
   You will learn to:

- recognize 20 fallacies commonly used in spoken and written communication,

- reserve judgment about the seriousness of fallacious thinking by the speaker,
- enter into a dialogue to help the speaker correct fallacies, and
- make a behavioral assessment of the speaker's level of fallacious thinking.

You will learn about types of logical fallacies: relevance fallacies, induction fallacies, formal fallacies, and fallacies of language. These fallacies include some that you have probably been warned about since you were young, for example, "Two wrongs don't make a right!" They also include more complex formal fallacies such as undistributed middle.

Grey Behaviors after Logical Fallacies in Public and Professional Communication analyzes behaviors occurring in dialogues between two fictional characters named Pat and Chris. Pat makes a claim which contains fallacious arguments. Chris gives feedback and tries to correct Pat's reasoning. Pat's reactions range from quick understanding and correction of the fallacy (light grey behavior) to failure to understand and then to compound multiple fallacies (dark grey behaviors). For each of 20 fallacies, we define the fallacy, give two examples, present four dialogues involving a third example, each followed by analysis of the degree of grey behavior expressed by Pat. Periodically, SELF-ASSESSMENTS are interspersed among the 20 fallacies to provide you chances to check your understanding.

Rhetorical devices, social influence techniques, and attributional biases are also described as other types of potentially misleading tactics. Along with logical fallacies, all these types of misleading tactics can interfere with effective communication. Studying this book will vaccinate you against the virus of misleading speech of others (identify, understand, and prevent fallacies).

Grey Behavior

Grey behavior is the reaction of the speaker to a listener's feedback. It starts with committing a fallacy, getting feedback from a listener, and then reacting. Four levels of grey behavior are introduced in this book, including Quick Correction, Being Convinced, Recurrence of the Fallacy, and Compounding of Fallacies.

Grey behavior is a way a person might distract or mislead you, so as to convince you to their way of thinking in an argument. Grey behavior is different from behaviors such as aggression. Aggression is the intentional infliction of harm on others (Branscombe & Baron, 2017), while grey behavior, as used in this book, is an effort to mislead others to convince them. The goal of aggression is to harm while the goal of grey behaviors is persuasion. Grey behavior starts with a bad argument called a fallacy. It may continue in reaction to the listener's feedback.

The speaker's behaviors in dialogues with others are analyzed in this book. Although a speaker may initially commit a fallacy, his or her subsequent behaviors after receiving feedback may be quite different. Four different patterns of behavior after receiving feedback include quickly correcting one's behavior, being convinced after additional feedback, repeating the fallacy, and even compounding subsequent fallacious behaviors.

Theoretical and Historical Background

There is a long history of the study of persuasion by philosophers, psychologists, and experts in decision-making and communication. According to Aristotle (2015) there are three modes of persuasion. First, we can be persuaded by a speaker's personal attributes, including such things as his or her background, reputation, accomplishments, or expertise. Aristotle referred to this mode of persuasion as ethos. Second, a speaker can persuade us by connecting with us on a personal level, or by arousing and appealing to our emotions by skillful use of rhetoric. This mode of persuasion Aristotle termed pathos. (Rhetoric is discussed more fully in Chapter 5. It may be a legitimate form of effective communication or, as used more recently, a manipulative diversion.) And third, the speaker may persuade us by using information and arguments including appeal to logic, reason, and facts, what he called logos (Moore & Parker, 2017). Box 1.1 provides a concise summary of Aristotle's analysis of persuasion.

Argument

In the classic usage, argument is not a pejorative term, as it is often used nowadays. Argument is simply an attempt to convince someone (possibly yourself) that a particular claim, called the conclusion, is true (Epstein, 2006, p. 5). We all do this every day. An

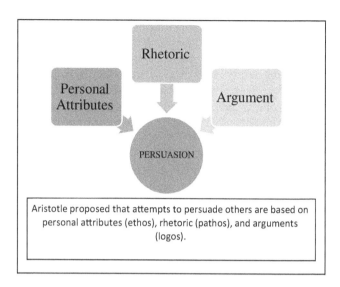

Box 1.1 Aristotle's Modes of Persuasion.

argument consists of two parts: One part gives a reason for accepting the second part (Moore & Parker, 2017, p. 7). This process is the basis for sound reasoning.

> Reasoning occurs whenever the mind draws conclusions on the basis of reasons. We draw conclusions whenever we make sense of things. Usually we are not aware of the full scope of reasoning in our lives. We begin to reason from the moment we wake up in the morning. We reason when we figure out what to eat for breakfast, what to wear, whether to stop at the store on the way to school, whether to go with this or that friend to lunch. We reason as we interpret the oncoming flow of traffic, when we react to the decisions of other drivers, when we speed up or slow down. We reason when we figure out solutions to problems. We reason when we formulate problems. We reason when we argue.
>
> (Paul & Elder, 2014, pp. 85–86)

Aristotle's articulation of the importance of reasoning provided the foundation for much Western philosophy. In addition, reasoning is one of the common elements of classical philosophy of not only ancient Greece, but also India and China (Baggini, 2018). In *How the World Thinks: A Global History of Philosophy*, Baggini explains that many philosophies throughout the world are based on the assumption that accurate logic is how to understand how the world works. He defines logic as the "systematic working through of the system of true statements (p. 54)." In the universe of situations, speakers try to convince others by reasoning with sound arguments. Listeners are supposed to be convinced by the speakers' arguments. As a listener you should avoid being misled by bad argument called Fallacy.

What Is Logical Fallacy (Bad Argument)?

There is a two-step process to the analysis, critique, and evaluation of an argument:

Step 1: Make sure the conclusion follows from the premise(s).
Step 2: Make sure all of the premises in the argument are true.

If either one of these conditions is absent, then the argument is bad and should be rejected. A fallacy has occurred when one thinks a conclusion follows from a premise when in fact it does not (Arp, Barbone, & Bruce, 2019, p. 28).

A logical fallacy is an argument that appears to be correct at first glance but is found to be incorrect in further examination. In a bad argument the premise doesn't support the contention.

Here is an example of a fallacy:

PARENT: *There is strong evidence of a link between smoking and chronic obstructive lung disease. Smoking is also associated with many other serious disorders. Smoking is unhealthy. So you should not smoke.*

CHILD: *But you smoke yourself. So much for your argument against smoking.*

Analysis: The **Child** committed the **Ad Hominem** fallacy by attacking the parent, but not by presenting any reason related to smoking (Walton, 1998, pp. 141–142). This argument is a fallacy – a mistake in reasoning.

Every day you are subject to influence techniques by other people such as advertisers on TV, political candidates, advocates of social causes, colleagues at work who want to persuade you of their ideas, and so on. For example, the following is a fallacious argument:

> I believe he made a terrible decision. Can you prove it isn't?

In this example, the speaker wants to convince you by using the bad argument called **Misplacing the Burden of Proof**. It's not your role to prove something *isn't* true; it's the speaker's obligation to prove his claim *is* true.

How can you avoid falling prey to bad arguments such as logical fallacies?

A Vaccine: The Purpose of Grey Behaviors after Logical Fallacies in Public and Professional Communication

Our aim of this relatively short book is to create a cognitive immunity for you when you are subjected by other peoples' attempts to convince you with bad arguments. We call the speaker's behavior "grey behaviors" because they can range from light to dark. When a speaker is seeking your attention and trying to be persuasive, you may fall prey to the speaker's bad arguments. If these arguments are fallacies, you may be misled. The knowledge of logical fallacies and the ability to identify bad arguments in the form of logical fallacies can make you immune to them. Identifying fallacies in the process of an argument is like identifying a virus in a medical diagnosis and injecting a vaccine. Vaccine makes our body's immune system stronger against viruses.

> A vaccine is a biological preparation that provides active acquired immunity to a particular infectious disease. A vaccine typically contains an agent that resembles a disease-causing microorganism and is often made from weakened or killed forms of the microbe, its toxins, or one of its surface proteins. The agent stimulates the body's immune system to recognize the agent as a threat, destroy it, and to further recognize and destroy any of the microorganisms associated with that agent that it may encounter in the future.
>
> (https://en.wikipedia.org/wiki/Vaccine)

There are many instances of liars in social history who misled others. For example, U.S. President Richard Nixon claimed that he knew nothing about a burglary in the offices of his political opponents. He did this so convincingly that he was re-elected. When his lies were uncovered, however, he resigned from office. Another example is Frank Abagnale, Jr. By the time he was 21, he had lied so convincingly that he persuaded others he was a lawyer, college professor, pediatrician, and an airline pilot.

> Perceiving others accurately is important for effective interaction. It is essential to know what people are really like beneath the public mask presented to the world and determine whether they are being honest with us about their motives. If we can't successfully assess whether people are trying to mislead us or not, we may find it difficult to interact effectively and build good relationships with them.
> (Branscombe & Baron, 2017, p. 91)

If you know about fallacies and explore the behaviors of the person who states them, you will immunize yourself against bad arguments. In this book we have two main goals.

• First, to help you understand and identify 20 logical fallacies and other influential tactics in an easy-to-understand text.
• Second, to provide a behavioral method to assess the degree of grey behavior the speaker shows after receiving feedback from you or other listeners. The speaker's reactions to feedback may show understanding, and we need not judge the person harshly. Or the speaker may persist with more grey behavior, and we are justified to conclude that the speaker may even be trying to mislead or lie to us.

Behavioral Assessors Should Know How to Evaluate Grey Behaviors

Formal situations such as recruitment interviews, performance reviews, assessment centers, situational judgment tests, and visa interviews are just a few places where assessors observe people's behaviors to evaluate analytical and critical thinking skills. For example, in the Analytical Writing and Discussion Test, verbal reports of reasoning by the examinee are assessed, and it is essential for assessors to know how to evaluate reasoning skills (Kord & Thornton, 2020).

In these situations, participants try to convince assessors. Participants naturally go all out to attract attention and make positive impressions. They often get coaching on how to do well and even pay for workshops to train them to show up well. Participants can become equipped with rhetorical devices, influence techniques, and other persuasive methods. Naturally, they come to the assessment process to put forth their best persuasive behaviors.

Thus, assessors need to be trained to be wary of fallacious thinking and how to assess the speaker's behavior after committing fallacies. This book will help you ferret out grey behaviors during such situations. It shows how to use a dialogue with the speaker to provide opportunities to dig deeper into the speaker's true reasoning abilities and motives. You will learn how to observe, record, classify, and rate speaker's behaviors. You will also have opportunities to do SELF ASSESSMENTS of your understanding.

It's important to know how to assess grey behaviors after a speaker first commits a fallacy.

When you first hear fallacy, you may suspect it is fallacious behavior, but more information is needed to make an accurate judgment about the speaker. If you give feedback, the speaker's reaction may differ greatly, and thus your assessment of these behaviors should differ. This process is important not only for behavioral assessors and psychologists but also for you in any situation where important matters are being discussed.

The process of evaluating the behaviors demonstrated by a person who receives feedback after speaking a fallacy must be accurate. In this book we apply many of the steps in the assessment center method (Thornton, Rupp, & Hoffman, 2015) to the challenge of assessing levels of fallacious thinking. Assessment centers have been proven to be reliable and valid over a long history of application in organizations around the world. In an assessment center, trained assessors observe behaviors relevant to well-defined management and leadership competencies, such as decision-making, interpersonal effectiveness, and communication. Observations are made in multiple standardized situational exercises which simulate relevant organizational challenges. Assessors watch for specific, overt behaviors known to be illustrative of positive and negative actions representative of the defined competencies. Assessors then evaluate the level of proficiency of each candidate using standardized rubrics. Assessment ratings are used to help make human resource decisions and to coach participants to increase competencies.

Similar processes are taught in this book to help you understand fallacious thinking. Several common fallacies are defined and everyday examples are provided so you understand what grey behaviors look like. Then an analysis is provided to show what "logical" behavior is. Dialogues between a speaker, Pat, and a listener, Chris, show examples of increasingly flagrant levels of fallacious behaviors. You will see both positive and negative behaviors in the dialogues. In other words, you will see examples of good reasoning and also bad reasoning related to the defined fallacies. Quizzes allow you to check your understanding of the processes.

If you want to assert that someone is not using sound reasoning, you need to give good evidence. Here are two observations you could make:

COMMENT 1: *Pat's conclusion sounds fishy because Pat didn't show enough evidence.*

COMMENT 2: *Pat's conclusion sounds fishy and sounds like a Hasty Generalization. The conclusion was based on just one isolated situation. Pat didn't follow up with an explanation with enough specific evidence. That was a fallacy in critical thinking, therefore Pat's argument is not convincing.*

Which comment was a better argument in evaluating Pat's behavior? Both state the same conclusion, "Pat's argument is fishy", but the arguments are different. The first is based on an opinion, but the second argues based on the valid reference and specified the kind of fallacy Pat committed. The second shows you have read the book *Grey Behaviors after Logical Fallacies in Public and Professional Communication*!

The behavioral assessment process you will learn here is based on sound argument. It helps you determine how the speaker's behaviors are good or bad and how to make a good conclusion about the speaker's fallacious thinking. Determinations of "good" or "bad" should not be based only on your opinions or general impressions; they should be based on logic. In this book, we describe bad arguments described in books on critical thinking. If you learn how to identify fallacies in a systematic way, you can give valid evidence in your assessment of grey behavior.

To achieve this goal, we collected logical errors from different leading critical thinking textbooks. We present definitions and examples, levels of grey behavior, and analyzes for 20 fallacies. Fallacies 1–9 describe fallacies which involve claims based on information that is not relevant to the conclusion. Fallacies 10–17 deal with inductive arguments in which arguments offer at best only weak support for their conclusions (Moore & Parker, 2017).

Fallacy 18 describes what experts call deductive arguments, that is, the premise (if true) proves the conclusion. Here the fallacy is that the premise does not prove the conclusion. Fallacy 19 involves ambiguous words. Finally, Fallacy 20 involves false statements of how parts of a situation and the whole situation are related to each other.

Why We Use the Title *Grey Behaviors*

The word **grey** refers to a color between very light to very dark. There is not a single grey color. There is a spectrum of grey colors ranging from nearly white to nearly black. For the purposes of scoring the degree of grey behaviors we arbitrarily chose just four levels: 1, 2, 3, 4.

In applications of process described in *Grey Behaviors after Logical Fallacies in Public and Professional Communication,* assessors observe and rate behaviors of people to assign a value to them. But when assessors face behaviors such as committing logical fallacies, using rhetoric or social influence techniques, or making attributions of people's behavior, they are not certain about values of these behaviors. At first sight, some behaviors such as using rhetoric devices seem positive in some occasions and negative in other occasions. Therefore, when assessors face these behaviors they should ask follow-up questions. After following up, assessors can understand what is beneath the behavior, analyze its intent, and form accurate assessment of the speaker.

Because of this uncertainty at first glance, we believe there is no single value for these behaviors. There is a spectrum of values from a basically logical behavior to a highly fallacious behavior. So, the title *Grey Behaviors after Logical Fallacies in Public and Professional Communication* brings to mind the association of something between logical and fallacious. We boil this down to levels 1, 2, 3, or 4.

In critical thinking textbooks you learn how to evaluate argument and how to diagnose bad arguments called fallacy. In these books, the authors never assess or analyze the speakers' behavior after committing fallacies. They just evaluate whether speakers' reasons support their claim, which means that in critical thinking books they evaluate propositions not behaviors.

In this book you learn not only to diagnose fallacies but also to assess speakers' behaviors after committing fallacies. Grey behaviors occur in a dialogue and not monologue. In a dialogue, there is a listener who gives feedback to the speaker and the speaker continues his/her argument in response to the listener's feedback. This dialogue goes on to get a result such as being convinced, conflicted, or ending of the dialogue. Thus, there is not a single mode of behavior. Rather, there is a series of the speaker's behaviors so that we can observe a trend of the speaker's behavior from committing a fallacy at the start of dialogue, getting the feedback from the listener, the speaker's response to the listener's feedback, and so on.

One approach is to assign a zero-one value to an argument whether it is good or bad. With this zero-one approach we can say an argument is a fallacy because reasons don't support the claim or evidence is not enough. This is what occurs in most critical thinking books.

We advocate a different approach. We believe it is more informative and helpful to gather information about the speaker's thinking. So this book shows how to assess the speaker's behavior in a dialogue. It takes into consideration the speaker's behavior in response to the listener's feedback. For example, suppose that speaker 1 and speaker 2 both commit the same fallacy but their behaviors are different after getting feedback from the listener. Speaker 1 may readily correct his/her argument after getting feedback, but speaker 2 may repeat his/her fallacy again. Although they both committed the same fallacy at the start of the dialogue, their responses to the feedbacks were different. In this case, we can use the Grey behavior assessment method to assess their behaviors, understand their reasoning, and thus their intentions.

Yes, grey behaviors may distract or mislead us, and some people may be deceived. In this dark space, it is important to provide a torch for assessors to at least recognize these misleading behaviors and prepare to face them. Therefore, this book can help assessors learn how to assess people after committing fallacies more accurately.

Grey Assessment Process

At first glance, what a speaker says may be a fallacy, but the degree of fallaciousness in the person's behavior can differ widely.

This degree can be assessed through a dialogue between you and the speaker. When a speaker commits a fallacy, you can give feedback and ask to get more information. The speaker's reactions to your feedback may differ as following:

1   The speaker corrects the fallacy immediately after getting feedback and changes the argument.
2   The speaker asks for your viewpoint. You clarify the fallacy and the speaker changes the position after learning from you.
3   The speaker repeats the fallacy, doesn't commit other kinds of fallacies, but persists on committing the first fallacy again.
4   The speaker compounds the fallacies. You clarify the fallacy, but the speaker doesn't accept your viewpoint, and states a combination of different kinds of fallacies to try to convince you.

If you observe each of the above you can evaluate grey behavior as following:

1	2	3	4
Quick-correction	Convinced	Recurrence	Compound

This grey spectrum shows that the degree of a grey behavior is different and depends on the speaker's reaction. When you observe a grey behavior you should not make a hasty judgment. You should do the following steps to evaluate the speaker's behavior:

Step 1: Listen to the speaker carefully and determine what kind of fallacy he or she has committed.
Step 2: Give feedback to and ask the speaker to give more information.
Step 3: Observe the reactions the speaker shows.
Step 4: Assign a grey degree to speaker's behavior.

The degree of a grey behavior the speaker commits depends on their reactions to listener's feedback.

Here is an example of dialogue between Pat and Chris. This example has been presented in four states that show degrees of grey behavior. These two characters are with you throughout this book in all chapters. Pat is always the person who commits fallacies and Chris is the listener who gives feedback. Pat's first sentence is a fallacy. Chris offers feedback. Pat shows different behaviors in the dialogues.

Dialogue 1: Pat and Chris are talking about whether waterboarding is torture.				
PAT: *You think waterboarding is torture? That sounds like something those left-wing college professors would say.* CHRIS: *Please tell me about waterboarding not left-wing college professors.* PAT: Oh, yes. I think that waterboarding is not torture because … reason 1 … reason 2….				
Grey Assessment State: Quick-correction **Grey Degree**: 1	1	2	3	4

Analysis: At first, Pat attacks left-wing professors rather than focusing on the subject. Pat goes the right direction immediately after getting feedback. This behavior is evaluated as a grey behavior with degree of 1 (its color is quite light). If we want to evaluate Pat's behavior only on the first argument: *"You think waterboarding is torture? That sounds like something those left-wing college professors would say"* we identify it as a fallacy from the view of logic, as **Argumentum ad Hominem** fallacy (chapter 1, fallacy 1), but when Pat comes into a dialogue, that behavior is corrected immediately. This is an important observation to assess Pat's behaviors. This is why we label grey to such behaviors. In the next dialogues, we can see another kind of grey behavior.

Dialogue 2				
PAT: *You think waterboarding is torture? That sounds like something those left-wing college professors would say.* CHRIS: *Please tell me about waterboarding, not left-wing college professors.* PAT: *Left-wings are the people who talk about it always. We cannot ignore them. What do you think?* CHRIS: *Maybe. But we should concentrate on problem not on people. Waterboarding is problem and what's your point of view. Do you think it is a torture?* PAT: *Ok. I think that Waterboarding is not torture because …*				
Grey Assessment State: Convinced **Grey Degree**: 2	1	2	3	4

Analysis: Pat committed a fallacy, then got feedback and learned from Chris, and is convinced. We don't evaluate Pat's opinion about waterboarding; we only assess the argument and behaviors not opinions. Grey degree of Pat's behavior is 2.

Dialogue 3
PAT: *You think waterboarding is torture? That sounds like something those left-wing college professors would say.* **CHRIS**: *Please tell me about waterboarding, not left-wing college professors.* **PAT**: *Left-wings are the people who talk about it always. We cannot ignore them.* **CHRIS**: *Maybe. But we should concentrate on problem not on people. Waterboarding is problem and what's your viewpoint? Do you think it is a torture?* **PAT**: *You repeat that opinion because you are proponent of left-wings.*
Grey Assessment **State**: Recurrence **Grey Degree**: 3   1 2 3 4

Analysis: Pat committed a fallacy and repeated it after his discussion with Chris. Grey degree of Pat's behavior is 3.

Dialogue 4
PAT: *You think waterboarding is torture? That sounds like something those left-wing college professors would say.* **CHRIS**: *Please tell me about waterboarding, not left-wing college professors.* **PAT**: *Do you think that Professors' viewpoints are not important?* **CHRIS**: *No! I didn't say it. I mean we should concentrate on problem, not on people.* **PAT**: *But they are people who cause a problem.* **CHRIS**: *Our issue was waterboarding, and we should explain it. Please don't talk about left-wings or right-wings.* **PAT**: *I didn't talk about left and right. That was you who just said left-wings and right-wings. Didn't you say that?*
Grey Assessment **State**: Compound **Grey Degree**: 4   1 2 3 4

Analysis: In the fourth dialogue, Pat committed a fallacy, didn't show learning, repeated the fallacy and committed a different kind of fallacy. Pat attacked to left-wing professors at first, as a fallacy of **Argumentum ad Hominem**, then misrepresented Chris's viewpoint and committed Strawman fallacy (chapter 1, fallacy 2), then Pat denied and attacked to Chris. This was a compound grey behavior which is the worst grey behavior.

Applications of Grey Degree Scores

Each individual score, after conducting a dialogue, provides an assessment of how the speaker behaves in reasoning with a particular topic in a dialogue. By combining the scores from dialogues of several topics, an overall assessment of argumentative skills can be obtained. Later parts of the book will describe a variety of practical and research applications of overall fallacious thinking.

Reading this book will provide the following benefits:

1   Behavioral assessors, psychologists, and others will learn 20 fallacies and logical errors by reading a simple book without having to read philosophical textbooks or critical thinking textbooks.
2   Making the behavioral assessor's conclusion a good argument by referencing the given errors which form a valid reference.
3   Learning how to assess the speaker's reactions to the listener's feedback after the speaker commits a logical error.
4   Learning the grey assessment process.
5   Enabling research by generating data to do correlation or causality studies between logical fallacies, grey behaviors, and personality traits for researchers of cognitive, social, clinical, or organizational psychology.
6   A guideline for identifying developmental needs of critical thinking skills.

⚠ Caution

This symbol of Caution is shown to warn readers not to over-interpret what the book can accomplish. Do not infer that the numbers from the assessment of the degree of grey behavior reflect an accurate assessment of change in the listener. The speaker assigned an assessment of "1" may just be voicing agreement to be compliant and putting an end to the dialogue. In other words, the speaker may not be "de-biased" with regard to the fallacious thinking or other grey behaviors just expressed.

On the dark grey end, the behaviors resulting in an assessment of "4" may be only momentarily defiant in the heat of the argument, yet really experience change in understanding. A positive result of the dialogue may be a "late hit," which shows up subsequently in the person's thinking and communication.

In summary, the caution sign is meant to inject a disclaimer. Human interactions and communication are complex. A few minutes of reading short dialogues may not provide an accurate assessment of the true state of the other person's beliefs, nor a change in behavior in the future.

Logical Fallacies

In the next three chapters, we define and illustrate 20 logical fallacies.

For each fallacy,

- We give the name of a fallacy.
- We give a definition.
- We give two examples in everyday life.
- We give a third example with four dialogues between Pat and Chris showing different levels of Pat's grey behavior.
- We give an analysis of each behavior of the speaker and the rationale for the assessment of the severity of the grey behavior.

The three chapters contain a cluster of fallacies. Each cluster consists of fallacies, which have similar features or a common element in the misuse of argument, logic, or wording.

Chapter 2 Grey Behaviors after Relevance Fallacies 1–9

In a Relevance fallacy, its premise is not relevant to the issue in question. In other words, a person committing a relevance fallacy says something or asks a question that is not relevant to the topic being discussed. Another label could be "lack of relevance" in the reasoning of the speaker.

Chapter 3 Grey Behaviors after Fallacies of Induction 10–17

In fallacies of Induction, arguments that are supposed to raise the probability of their conclusions are so weak as to fail almost entirely to do so. In other words, in these fallacies a person uses a small number of selected cases to form a conclusion. Another label could be "too few observations" in the reasoning of the speaker.

Chapter 4 Grey Behaviors after Formal Fallacies and Fallacies of Language 18–20

Formal fallacies result from a failure of form, which refers to the way the argument is set up. In other words, in Formal fallacies the form of the argument itself is invalid. Fallacies of Language contain misuse of language. In other words, in fallacies of Language the speaker uses vague or ambiguous words. The reason is words such as "they say."

Guidance for Assessment of the Degree of Grey Behavior

Pat and Chris are discussing some topic in the following four dialogues. In each dialogue, Pat shows a degree of grey behavior. Pat shows Quick Correction behavior in Dialogue 1, a behavior of being Convinced in Dialogue 2, behavior showing Recurrence of the logical error in Dialogue 3, and the worst grey behavior in Dialogue 4 in which Compound fallacies are shown. The subject of four dialogues is the same but Pat's behaviors vary from dialogue to dialogue. Read the dialogues carefully and pay attention to Pat's reactions to Chris. These reactions determine the degree of grey behavior in each dialogue. The last row of each dialogue box is the result of assessment of Pat's grey behavior. Degree 1 indicates that Pat commits a fallacy first but immediately corrects it after getting feedback from Chris (Quick-correction). Degree 2 indicates that Pat commits a fallacy again but is Convinced after getting feedback and some discussion with Chris. Grey behavior is worse than Degree 1. Degree 3 indicates that Pat commits a fallacy and repeats it even after feedback; this shows the Recurrence of the same fallacy. Degree 4 indicates that Pat commits a Compound of fallacies, which means a set of different fallacies in reaction to continuing feedback from Chris. The fourth degree is the worst grey behavior that Pat shows in the four dialogues.

Periodically, we provide SELF ASSESSMENTS. They are self-tests that provide you chances to test your understanding of fallacies.

⚠ **Caution!**

Communication is complex. Short dialogues may not change the speaker, listener, or reader.

---

2 Grey Behaviors after Relevance Fallacies 1–9

In this chapter,

- We analyze nine relevance fallacies defined in books by leading authorities.
- We give two examples from everyday life.
- We present a set of four dialogues in which Pat states a fallacious argument, Chris provides feedback, and Pat replies with differing levels of grey behavior.
- After each of Pat's responses, we give our analysis of what the bad argument was.

After Fallacy 4 and Fallacy 9, you will have opportunities to complete a SELF-ASSESSMENT to check your level of understanding of the fallacies and the method of assessing the level of grey behavior following the fallacy.

Fallacy 1 Ad Hominem (Personal Attack)

"An *ad hominem* argument rejects or dismisses another person's statement by attacking the person rather than the statement itself" (Kelley, 2014, p. 113).

The following are two examples from different critical thinking books.

Example 1.1

Team meeting in a hospital.

SOCIAL WORKER TO PSYCHIATRIST: "Could you clarify how you are using the term bipolar personality disorder?"

PSYCHIATRIST: "I always wondered what they teach you at Berkeley, and now I can see it's not much."

Analysis: The **Psychiatrist** attacked the **Social Worker**, but didn't clarify how he was using the term bipolar personality disorder (Gambrill & Gibbs, 2017, p. 168).

Example 1.2

Two government officials are discussing the need for personal identity cards.

OFFICIAL ONE: "Personal identity cards are an infringement of individual human rights."

OFFICIAL TWO: "Identity cards don't present any real dangers to human rights. They add to our security, by making it easier for the police to track and catch criminals. Opponents of identity cards are wishy-washy liberals who live in leafy areas and haven't a clue what it is like to live in run-down areas where crime is rife."

Analysis: Official Two attacks everyone who opposes the introduction of identity cards on personal terms like "wishy-washy liberals." It also makes unsubstantiated assumptions about the backgrounds and economic circumstances of opponents, in order to undermine their credibility. The passage relies on attacks on the speaker rather than reasons and evidence, and thus demonstrates **Ad Hominem** fallacy in reasoning (Cottrell, 2005, p. 117, passage 7.18).

Example 1.3: Dialogues

In the following four separate dialogues, Pat displays increasing degrees of Grey Behavior. Read each dialogue carefully and assess the degree of Grey Behavior. The analysis following each dialogue explains the rationale and assigns a degree of Grey Behavior. Degree 1 indicates Pat commits a fallacy, but shows a Quick Correction after getting feedback from Chris. Degree 2 indicates Pat accepts that the statements are faulty and is convinced of committing a fallacy. Degree 3 indicates Pat commits a fallacy and shows a Recurrence of the same fallacy a second time even after more feedback from Chris. Degree 4 indicates Pat commits Compound fallacies.

Example 1.3_Dialogue 1: Two human resource managers are discussing an incident in their company. Pat and Chris are evaluating a recommendation about alleged theft in their company.

PAT: *I would not agree to Mary's recommendation to fire Ann, because Mary does not like Ann's sexual orientation.*

CHRIS: Please tell me about Mary's recommendation not Mary's opinions.

PAT: *You are right. I don't agree to this recommendation because Mary has not provided evidence of a theft.*

Grey Assessment
State: Quick Correction **Grey Degree**: 1

1	2	3	4

Analysis: In this dialogue **Pat** first committed fallacy of **Ad Hominem** but corrects the argument after listening to **Chris's** feedback. Because of this, we can assess **Pat's** behavior as grey behavior but the state of this behavior is **Quick Correction** and degree of Grey Behavior is 1 which means that his behavior is a little fallacious.

Example 1.3_Dialogue 2

PAT: *I would not agree to Mary's recommendation to fire Ann because Mary does not like Ann's sexual orientation.*

CHRIS: *Please tell me about Mary's recommendation, not Mary's opinions.*

PAT: *But this is her recommendation and her opinions may have affected her recommendation.*

CHRIS: *Maybe! But you should concentrate on the recommendation's weakness and strength, not on the person who came up with it.*

PAT: *OK! The weakness of this recommendation is Mary did not provide evidence of a theft.*

Grey Assessment
State: Convinced **Grey Degree**: 2

1	2	3	4

Analysis: In the second dialogue **Pat** didn't correct the **Ad Homi-nem** fallacious behavior immediately but was **Convinced** after some more discussion and recognized the weakness. Degree of the grey behavior is 2 which means that it took two arguments to get **Pat** to admit the weakness.

Example 1.3_Dialogue 3
PAT: *I would not agree to Mary's recommendation to fire Ann because Mary does not like Ann's sexual orientation.* **CHRIS**: *Please tell me about Mary's recommendation, not Mary's opinions.* **PAT**: *But this is her recommendation and her opinions may have been affected her recommendation.* **CHRIS**: *Maybe! But you should concentrate on the recommendation's weakness and strength not on the person who have come up with it.* **PAT**: *I know that Mary is jealous of Ann! And she should not give any recommendation to fire Ann.*
Grey Assessment **State**: Recurrence **Grey Degree**: 3   1 | 2 | 3 | 4

Analysis: In the third dialogue **Pat** first committed the **Ad Hominem** argument and after some discussion returned to the first position and repeated committing this fallacy again. This **Recurrence** of grey in this behavior is worse than the behavior in the two first dialogues, so the degree of Grey Behavior is 3.

Example 1.3_Dialogue 4
PAT: *I would not agree to Mary's recommendation to fire Ann because Mary does not like Ann's sexual orientation.* **CHRIS**: *Please tell me about Mary's recommendation, not Mary's opinions.* **PAT**: *But this is her recommendation and her opinions may have affected her recommendation.* **CHRIS**: *Maybe! But you should concentrate on the recommendation's weakness and strength, not on the person who have come up with it.* **PAT**: *Perhaps you are on her side!* **CHRIS**: *No. Suppose that someone else has come up with this recommendation. How do you assess it?* **PAT**: *I don't know what you mean? Are you evaluating me? Do you want to say that you know better than me …*
Grey Assessment **State**: Compound **Grey Degree**: 4   1 | 2 | 3 | 4

Analysis: In the fourth dialogue **Pat** first committed fallacy of **Ad Hominem**. After discussion, **Pat** not only didn't correct the first argument but also committed a **Strawman** fallacy by saying **Chris** is "evaluating me" and "you are better than me." Two fallacies are **Compounded.** So the degree of grey behavior is 4, which means that the behavior in the dialogue is the worst among all the dialogues.

Fallacy 2 Straw Man

"The **Straw Man** fallacy is committed when a person distorts or misrepresents the opponent's argument, thus making it easier to knock it down or refute it. This tactic is particularly common in political rhetoric over controversial issues" (Boss, 2017, p. 150).

Example 2.1

PERSON1: It would be bad for the environment to increase emissions by developed countries.

PERSON2: How can you say that? Stopping the economic growth rate is what you want!

Analysis: Person2's feedback (economic growth) is a fallacious argument because it misrepresents the argument (environment) of **Person1**.

Example 2.2

PERSON1: I want to find a new job in another city.

PERSON2: Do you mean that you are not satisfied with your current job?

Analysis: Person2's feedback (job satisfaction) is a fallacious argument, because it misrepresents the proposition (desire for new job) of **Person1**.

Example 2.3: Dialogues

In the following four separate dialogues Pat displays increasing degrees of Grey Behavior. Read each dialogue carefully and assess the degree of Grey Behavior. The analysis following each dialogue explains the rationale and assigns a degree of Grey Behavior. Degree 1 indicates Pat commits a fallacy, but shows a Quick Correction after getting feedback from Chris. Degree 2 indicates Pat accepts that the statements are faulty and is Convinced of committing a fallacy. Degree 3 indicates Pat commits a fallacy and shows a Recurrence of the same fallacy a second time even after more feedback from Chris. Degree 4 indicates Pat commits Compound fallacies.

Example 2.3_Dialogue 1: A group of faculty at a university is discussing causes of aggression. Pat and Chris are talking about gender differences in aggression.
CHRIS: *The recent data from Canada indicate that men are much more likely than women to engage in crimes involving aggression.* **PAT**: *Do you mean that I'm aggressive?* **CHRIS**: *No, I just said that a research in Canada showed that men are more aggressive than women. It's not about you. Please tell me your opinion about gender differences in aggression.* **PAT**: *OK! I think so! Yes, this claim is based on research data. It is important to get more data around the world ….*
Grey Assessment **State**: Quick Correction **Grey Degree**: 1   1 2 3 4

Analysis: In the first dialogue **Pat** committed a **Straw Man** fallacy, accusing **Chris** of saying **Pat** is aggressive, but quickly **Corrected** the argument. Degree of grey behavior is 1.

Example 2.3_Dialogue 2
CHRIS: *The recent data from Canada indicate that men are much more likely than women to engage in crimes involving aggression.* **PAT**: *Do you mean that I'm aggressive?* **CHRIS**: *No, I just said that a research in Canada showed that men are more aggressive than women. It's not about you. Please tell me your opinion about gender differences in aggression.* **PAT**: *But I'm a member of the men group. If it is true about men, it would be true about me too.* **CHRIS**: *Maybe! It shows that men as a whole have done such behavior way more than women, and it does not show that every man is more aggressive than every woman. It's likely you can find some women who are more aggressive than some men. But in total the research data are true.* **PAT**: *OK! It would be better to get more data around the world.*
Grey Assessment **State**: Convinced **Grey Degree**: 2   1 2 3 4

Analysis: Pat committed **Straw Man** fallacy, but after more discussion is **Convinced** to come to the right position, that is, the need for data. Degree of Grey Behavior is 2.

Example 2.3_Dialogue 3

CHRIS: *The recent data from Canada indicate that men are much more likely than women to engage in crimes involving aggression.*
PAT: *Do you mean that I'm aggressive?*
CHRIS: *No, I just said that a research in Canada showed that men are more aggressive than women. It's not about you. Please tell me your opinion about gender differences in aggression.*
PAT: *But I'm a member of the men group. If it is true about men It would be true about me too.*
CHRIS: *Maybe! It shows that men as a whole have done such way more than women and it does not show that every man is more aggressive than every woman. It's likely you can find some women who are more aggressive than some men but in total the research data are true.*
PAT: *Do you mean that you know every man and woman?*

Grey Assessment	
State: Recurrence **Grey Degree**: 3	

Analysis: Pat committed a **Straw Man** fallacy ("Do you mean I'm aggressive?) and after an exchange persisted in the first position and restated a **Straw Man** fallacy ("you know every man and woman). Degree of grey behavior is 3, which means that the behavior is worse than the two previous dialogues.

Example 2.3_Dialogue 4

CHRIS: *The recent data from Canada indicate that men are much more likely than women to engage in crimes involving aggression.*
PAT: *Do you mean that I'm aggressive?*
CHRIS: *No, I just said that a research in Canada showed that men are more aggressive than women. It's not about you. Please tell me your opinion about gender differences in aggression.*
PAT: *Dealing with such researches supports inequality. I don't want to participate in this activity.*
CHRIS: *It's important for us to know similarities and differences between men and women, and doing such things doesn't mean that we support inequality. Inequality means that we unfairly support men or women. This research has fairly done.*
PAT: *You are advocating feminism!*

Grey Assessment	
State: Compound **Grey Degree**: 4	

Analysis: At first, **Pat** committed **Straw Man** fallacy, then stated an irrelevant conclusion, and at last committed an **Ad Hominem** argument ("advocating feminism"). The degree of Grey Behavior is 4, which means that the behavior is even more fallacious.

Fallacy 3 False Dilemma

"The **False Dilemma** fallacy happens when someone tries to establish a conclusion by offering it as the only alternative to something most people will find unacceptable, unattainable, or implausible" (Moore & Parker, 2017, p. 177).

The fallacy is committed when a speaker or writer gives an argument which reduces the number of alternatives to two: "perfection" and "nothing."

Example 3.1

Drilling for oil in the Gulf won't give us independence from OPEC; therefore, we shouldn't drill.

Analysis: This speaker tries to establish that we should not drill in the Gulf. She ignores the less-than-perfect possibility that drilling for oil in the Gulf could make us less dependent on OPEC (Moore & Parker, 2017, p. 178).

Example 3.2

America—love it or leave it! If you don't like U.S. policy, then move somewhere else!

Analysis: That **False Dilemma** argument makes the unwarranted assumption that the only alternative to accepting U.S. policies is to move to another country. In fact, there are many alternatives, including working to change or improve U.S. policies (Boss, 2017, p. 154).

Example 3.3: Dialogues

In the following four separate dialogues, Pat displays increasing degrees of Grey Behavior. Read each dialogue carefully and assess the degree of Grey Behavior. The analysis following each dialogue explains the rationale and assigns a degree of Grey Behavior. Degree 1 indicates Pat commits a fallacy, but shows a Quick Correction after getting feedback from Chris. Degree 2 indicates that Pat accepts the statements as faulty and is convinced of committing a fallacy. Degree 3 indicates Pat commits a fallacy and shows a Recurrence of the same fallacy a second time even after more feedback from Chris. Degree 4 indicates Pat commits Compound fallacies.

Example 3.3_Dialogue 1: In a community-sponsored program on healthy lifestyles, Pat and Chris are talking about whitening teeth.

PAT: *Save your money. Nothing will make your teeth perfectly white.*
CHRIS: *They do not have to be perfectly white.*
PAT: *Yes. It would be useful to clean your teeth partly.*

Grey Assessment				
State: Quick Correction **Grey Degree**: 1	1	2	3	4

Analysis: Pat commits a **False Dilemma** fallacy by saying *"nothing"* will make teeth perfectly white, so save your money. **Pat** is suggesting white teeth are unattainable so don't try. **Chris** points out that a person doesn't have to have perfectly white teeth. **Pat** acknowledges the usefulness of partially clean teeth. This shows **Quick-correction** and the score is 1.

Example 3.3_Dialogue 2

PAT: *Save your money. Nothing will make your teeth perfectly white.*
CHRIS: *They do not have to be perfectly white.*
PAT: *But cleaning partly does not assure your teeth becoming white.*
CHRIS: *Yes but it at least can help make them better than before or reducing risk of becoming worse.*
PAT: *OK.*

Grey Assessment				
State: Convinced **Grey Degree**: 2	1	2	3	4

Analysis: After the first exchange, **Pat** continues to call for an unattainable result. **Pat** is finally **Convinced** with **Chris'** additional statement of the benefit of cleaning, and thus the score is 2.

Example 3.3_Dialogue 3

PAT: *Save your money. Nothing will make your teeth perfectly white.*
CHRIS: *It does not have to be perfectly white.*
PAT: *Isn't your goal making your teeth white?*
CHRIS: *Yes, but it at least can help make it better than before or reducing risk of becoming worse.*
PAT: *If it doesn't assure making your teeth white you're wasting your money.*

Grey Assessment				
State: Recurrence **Grey Degree**: 3	1	2	3	4

Analysis: Here **Pat** is restating the **False Dilemma** by saying if whitening doesn't make the teeth white, it is wasting money. Score of 3 for a **Recurring** fallacy.

Example 3.3_Dialogue 4
PAT: *Save your money. Nothing will make your teeth perfectly white.* **CHRIS**: *It does not have to be perfectly white.* **PAT**: *Isn't your goal making your teeth white?* **CHRIS**: *Yes, but it at least can help make it better than before or reducing risk of becoming worse.* **PAT**: *You're kind of person who go all out to appear more attractive than you are!* **CHRIS**: *We are talking about making teeth white not any desire I may have about my appearance.* **PAT**: *Do you mean I'm mistaken?*
Grey Assessment   **State**: Compound **Grey Degree**: 4   1 2 3 4

Analysis: Here **Pat** compounds the **False Dilemma** fallacy by committing another fallacy, the **Ad Hominem** fallacy, in stating "you're the kind of person," but not by addressing the value of whitening one's teeth and finally **Pat** committed **Straw Man** in stating "Do you mean I'm mistaken?". Therefore, the degree of **Pat**'s behavior is 4.

Fallacy 4 Misplacing the Burden of Proof

"This fallacy is also called **Appeal to Ignorance**: An argument that something is true simply because no one has proved it false, or that something is false simply because no one has proved it true" (Boss, 2017, p. 148).

> If your doctor says you are infected with West Nile virus, you may ask, "Doctor, what makes you think that?" If she says, "What makes you think you aren't?" you will get a new doctor. Her remark is absurd because it is *her* job to tell you why she thinks you are infected with West Nile, not *your* job to tell her why you think you aren't. As this case, sometimes the burden of proof clearly falls more heavily on one side than another. When people try to support or prove their position by placing the burden to prove something is not true on someone else, they commit the fallacy called **Misplacing the Burden of Proof.**
>
> (Moore & Parker, 2017, p. 179)

Example 4.1

> I do not have much information on this except the general state-ment of the agency that there is nothing in the files to disprove his Communist connections.
>
> Senator Joe McCarthy

Analysis: McCarthy's point is to show that someone is a commu-nist based on the lack of evidence that he is *not* a communist. This maneuver in an argument commits the **Appeal to Ignorance** fallacy (McCraw, 2018, p. 106).

Example 4.2

JANE: *The existence of entities such as ghosts should be given no cre-dence whatsoever since there is no evidence that such things exist.*
JOHN: *Your skepticism is unwarranted. Science has never disproven the existence of ghosts.*

Analysis: John's reply assumes that it is **Jane** who incurs the **Burden of Proof** and that belief in ghosts is justified until some evidence against it is presented. But, in fact, the **Burden of Proof** lies with **John**. Although it is right that one cannot be certain that ghosts do not exist, it is **John** who has the burden of explaining why no one has ever been able to conduct a repeatable experiment with which to detect the existence of paranormal entities (Russo, 2018, p. 138).

Example 4.3: Dialogues

In the following four separate dialogues, Pat displays increasing degrees of Grey Behavior. Read each dialogue carefully and assess the degree of Grey Behavior. The analysis following each dialogue explains the rationale and assigns a degree of Grey Behavior. Degree 1 indicates Pat commits a fallacy, but shows a Quick Correction after getting feedback from Chris. Degree 2 indicates Pat accepts that the statements are faulty and is convinced of committing a fallacy. Degree 3 indicates Pat commits a fallacy and shows a Recurrence of the same fallacy a second time even after more feedback from Chris. Degree 4 indicates Pat commits Compound fallacies.

Example 4.3_Dialogue 1: In an on-line chat room, which is part of virtual lecture series on spooky books, Pat and Chris are talking about the existence of ghosts.

PAT: *Nobody has proved ghosts don't exist; therefore they do.*
CHRIS: *You should have given evidence of their existence.*
PAT: *I don't have any evidence. So, I cannot show they exist or not.*

Grey Assessment	
State: Quick Correction **Grey Degree**: 1	

Analysis: Pat committed the fallacy of **Misplacing the Burden of Proof** by stating someone else needs to prove ghosts do not exist, when in fact the burden of proof falls on **Pat** to claim they do exist. After **Chris** states that **Pat** has the burden, **Pat Corrects** the position and the score is 1.

Example 4.3_Dialogue 2

PAT: *Nobody has proved ghosts don't exist; therefore they do.*
CHRIS: *You should have given evidence of their existence.*
PAT: *I don't have any evidence. But there is no evidence that ghosts don't exist.*
CHRIS: *When you don't have any evidence you shouldn't make a conclusion.*
PAT: *OK. You're right.*

Grey Assessment	
State: Convinced **Grey Degree**: 2	1 2 3 4

Analysis: When **Chris** says for a second time that **Pat** needs evidence to claim ghosts exist, **Pat** says OK. This shows **Pat** understands and is **Convinced**, scored 2.

Example 4.3_Dialogue 3
PAT: *Nobody has proved ghosts don't exist; therefore they do.* CHRIS: *You should have given evidence of their existence.* PAT: *I don't have any evidence personally. But there is no evidence that ghosts don't exist.* CHRIS: *When you don't have any evidence you shouldn't conclude.* PAT: *But I believe that they exist. Show me I'm wrong!*

Grey Assessment State: Recurrence **Grey Degree**: 3	1	2	3	4

Analysis: Pat is repeatedly **Misplacing the Burden of Proof** on someone else to provide evidence ghosts do not exist. This is a **Recurrence** of the fallacy, and is scored 3.

Example 4.3_Dialogue 4
PAT: *Nobody has proved ghosts don't exist; therefore they do.* CHRIS: *You should have given evidence of their existence.* PAT: *It's not my task to gather evidence!* CHRIS: *I mean if everybody wants to show that something exists, he or she has to bring evidence. Evidence makes your claim objective.* PAT: *You express as if you know everything. This is showing off!*

Grey Assessment State: Compound **Grey Degree**: 4	1	2	3	4

Analysis: After doubling down on **Misplacing the Burden of Proof** that someone else needs to prove ghosts do not exist or they really do exist, **Pat** then impugns **Chris'** character: you think you "know everything" and you are "showing off." These are **Ad Hominem** fallacies. These statements **Compound Pat's** fallacious behavior, a level 4 Grey Behavior.

SELF-ASSESSMENT 1

Now that you have learned about the first four logical fallacies, complete the following quizzes to check your understanding.

Quiz 1.1

Here are examples of the first four fallacies. After each example, write the letter for the fallacy in the space provided.

Examples	Fallacies
1. **Chris**: Does your job earn more money than before you got it? **Pat**: Do you mean that I have abused my position? ____	a) Argumentum Ad Hominem b) Straw Man c) False Dilemma d) Misplacing the Burden of Proof
2. If you don't accept my claim, show me it's wrong. ____	
3. If you want to be successful, you have to get a university degree. ____	
4. You are supporting this proposal because you have interest in this project. ____	

Quiz 1.2

The following monologue contains four fallacies. In the space after each fallacy, write the name of the fallacy. Then state what response you would make if you could speak to Pat.

> **Monologue. In a campaign speech for public office, candidate Pat says:**
> The ruling party has never done anything perfectly. They must be replaced now. ____ They say it is difficult to reach an agreement with the European Union this year. They mean we are not able to get any agreement. ____ But I'm here to show that, in contrast with them, we are capable of doing anything. ____ We can get the highest economic growth rate in the world and if they don't believe us, I tell them: can you prove we can't? ____

Quiz 1.3

Read the dialogue and indicate the state and degree of Grey Behavior.

Dialogue between Pat and Chris about Pat's monologue.				
PAT: How was my speech? **CHRIS**: *You committed four fallacies!* PAT: You don't want me to win the race. **CHRIS**: *I would like you to win but not with bad arguments.* PAT: *You are in the side of the ruling party.*				
Grey Assessment **State**: .... **Grey Degree**:	1	2	3	4

Answers on page 117.

Fallacy 5 Begging the Question

"In **Begging the Question** fallacy, the conclusion is simply a rewording of a premise. By making the conclusion the same as the premise, we are assuming that the conclusion is true rather than offering proof for it. This fallacy is also known as **Circular Reasoning**" (Boss, 2017, p. 153).

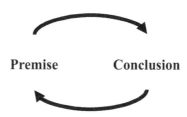

Premise   Conclusion

The fallacy here is that "A statement that is questionable as a conclusion is equally questionable as a premise" (Engel, 1994, p. 53).

Example 5.1

Obviously, the governor told the truth about the budget. He wouldn't lie to us about it.

Analysis: A speaker or writer is guilty of begging the question logically when he or she tries to "support" a contention by offering as "evidence" what amounts to a repackaging of the very contention in question (Moore & Parker, 2017, p. 182).

Example 5.2

Our products are the best in the world because they are highest in quality.

Analysis: Notice that the reason given restates the conclusion, but in different words.

Example 5.3: Dialogues

In the following four separate dialogues, Pat displays increasing degrees of Grey Behavior. Read each dialogue carefully and assess the degree of Grey Behavior. The analysis following each dialogue explains the rationale and assigns a degree of Grey Behavior. Degree 1 indicates Pat commits a fallacy, but shows a Quick Correction after getting feedback from Chris. Degree 2 indicates Pat accepts that the statements are faulty and is convinced of committing a fallacy. Degree 3 indicates Pat commits a fallacy and shows a Recurrence of the same fallacy a second time even after more feedback from Chris. Degree 4 indicates Pat commits Compound fallacies.

Example 5.3_Dialogue 1: At a social gathering Pat and Chris are talking about a mutual acquaintance.				
PAT: *She is trustworthy; after all, she swears she is, and you can't doubt that.* **CHRIS**: *Your claim is "she is trustworthy." But your supporting reason was rewording of your claim.* **PAT**: *Yes. I should find evidence.*				
Grey Assessment **State**: Quick Correction **Grey Degree**: 1	1	2	3	4

Analysis: Pat's statement is a clear case of **Circular Reasoning**. "She swears she is" is offered to support "she is trustworthy." **Pat Quick-corrects** by saying "I need evidence," thus showing mild Grey Behavior, 1.

Example 5.3_Dialogue 2				
PAT: *She is trustworthy; after all, she swears she is, and you can't doubt that.* **CHRIS**: *Your claim is "she is trustworthy." But your supporting reason was rewording of your claim.* **PAT**: *She swears she is.* **CHRIS**: *Your reason should have given evidence. Swearing is not evidence.* **PAT**: *Yes. I should find evidence.*				
Grey Assessment **State**: Convinced **Grey Degree**: 2	1	2	3	4

Analysis: Pat is **Convinced** after a second feedback from **Chris** that swearing to an assertion is not evidence. This is bit more Grey Behavior and is level 2.

Example 5.3_Dialogue 3
PAT: *She is trustworthy; after all, she swears she is, and you can't doubt that.* **CHRIS**: *Your claim is "she is trustworthy." But your supporting reason was rewording of your claim.* **PAT**: *She swears she is.* **CHRIS**: *Your reason should have given evidence. Swearing is not evidence.* **PAT**: *I trust her swearing.*
Grey Assessment **State**: Recurrence **Grey Degree**: 3

Analysis: Pat's trust in the person's swearing is little different from the earlier premises. Thus this is a **Recurrence** of **Circular Reasoning** and greyer than previous statements, and thus Degree 3.

Example 5.3_Dialogue 4
PAT: *She is trustworthy; after all, she swears she is, and you can't doubt that.* **CHRIS**: *Your claim is "she is trustworthy." But your supporting reason was rewording of your claim.* **PAT**: *She swears she is.* **CHRIS**: *Your reason should have given evidence. Swearing is not evidence.* **PAT**: *You don't trust anyone. Because you are skeptical of everything!* **CHRIS**: *You're attacking me. Also, the two sentences you have just said are rewording of each other. In this argument you didn't give evidence.* **PAT**: *You should change your approach because you always oppose me!*
Grey Assessment **State**: Compound **Grey Degree**: 4

Analysis: In addition to the fallacy of **Begging the Question**, **Pat** is making an **Ad Hominem** fallacy "You are skeptical of everything." The grey behaviors are duplicates and thus more serious, resulting in 4, the darkest grey.

Fallacy 6 Appeal to Emotion

"This fallacy is the attempt to persuade someone of a conclusion by an appeal to emotion instead of evidence. A person who commits this fallacy is hoping that his listeners will adopt a belief on the basis of a feeling he has instilled in them: outrage, hostility, fear, pity, guilt, or whatever" (Kelley, 2014, p. 106). This fallacy is also related to a rhetorical technique. See Chapter 5 for more rhetorical devices.

Example 6.1

Do you think Apple doesn't know it hires 12-year-old children to make its electronics? You think it isn't aware it pays them slave wages and has them work in buildings without heat or air conditioning? It knows. Apple products can't be any good.

The passage doesn't support the contention that Apple products aren't any good. Rather, it tries to *induce* us to have that belief by making us angry (Moore & Parker, 2017, p. 183).

Example 6.2

You really should get a Prudential life insurance policy. What would happen to your spouse and children if you die? Remember, you are their main source of income. Would they be forced to move? Prudential has really good policies!

This argument tries to scare you into buying a Prudential life insurance policy. But even if it is true that your spouse and children will be forced to move if you die, that is no reason to favor insurance from this particular company (Moore & Parker, 2017, p. 183).

Example 6.3: Dialogues

In the following four separate dialogues, Pat displays increasing degrees of Grey Behavior. Read each dialogue carefully and assess the degree of Grey Behavior. The analysis following each dialogue explains the rationale and assigns a degree of Grey Behavior. Degree 1 indicates Pat commits a fallacy, but shows a Quick Correction after getting feedback from Chris. Degree 2 indicates Pat accepts that the statements are faulty and is convinced of committing a fallacy. Degree 3 indicates Pat commits a fallacy and shows a Recurrence of the same fallacy a second time even after more feedback from Chris. Degree 4 indicates Pat commits Compound fallacies.

Example 6.3 Dialogue 1: At a family gathering Pat and Chris are talking about Chris's decision to buy a house.

PAT: *Why do you want to buy Fred's house? I remember he was repairing it last month. If it collapses, what would happen to you?*
CHRIS: *Don't frighten me! I saw his house and I think it is a good choice for me.*
PAT: *OK. You can get more information to make your decision.*

Grey Assessment	1	2	3	4
State: Quick Correction **Grey Degree**: 1				

Analysis: Pat uses the emotion of fear that the house will collapse to discourage **Chris** from buying the house. **Chris** saw the house and thinks it's a good choice, so **Pat** agrees and suggests **Chris** can get more information. This is a **Quick Correction** and only a mild Grey Behavior, Degree 1.

Example 6.4_Dialogue 2

PAT: *Why do you want to buy Fred's house? I remember he was repairing it last month. If it collapses, what would happen to you?*
CHRIS: *Don't scare me! I saw his house and I think It is a good choice for me.*
PAT: *I'm concerned and want your house to be safe.*
CHRIS: *Thank you. I will get more information before I make such an important decision.*
PAT: *OK.*

Grey Assessment	1	2	3	4
State: Convinced **Grey Degree**: 2				

Analysis: Chris says "Don't scare me!", thanks **Pat** for the concern for a safe house, and says more information will be sought. It takes all this before Pat realizes the **Appeal to Emotion** is not working and says OK. **Pat** is finally **Convinced**, but this level of dialogue was needed and thus is a higher level of Grey Behavior, Degree 2.

Example 6.4_Dialogue 3				
PAT: *Why do you want to buy Fred's house? I remember he was repairing it last month. If it collapses, what would happen to you?* **CHRIS**: *Don't scare me! I saw his house, and I think It is a good choice for me.* **PAT**: *I'm concerned and want your house to be safe.* **CHRIS**: *Thank you. I will get more information before I make such an important decision.* **PAT**: *If I were you I wouldn't endanger myself.*				
Grey Assessment State: Recurrence **Grey Degree**: 3	1	2	3	4

Analysis: Pat repeats the threat of the house collapsing with another **Appeal to Emotion** in the warning "I wouldn't endanger myself." This is a **Recurrence** of the fallacy of **Appeal to Emotion** and not real reasons for not buying the house. This is a Degree 3 of Grey Behavior.

Example 6.4_Dialogue 4				
PAT: *Why do you want to buy Fred's house? I remember he was repairing it last month. If it collapses, what would happen to you?* **CHRIS**: *I saw his house and I think It is a good choice for me. But I'll take your concern into consideration.* **PAT**: *Fred always argues with his wife and beats up his son sometimes. I think he is not qualified to negotiate!* **CHRIS**: *His private life is not relevant to our deal. It is an opportunity for me to buy this house, because it has a reasonable price and its location is very good. But I can get more information before signing the contract. Thank you.* **PAT**: *If I were you I wouldn't endanger myself. Why don't you buy my brother's? He needs money these days. If you buy it, his problems will be solved.* **CHRIS**: *I'm making decision to buy a house. Your brother's problems aren't relevant to my decision. We can talk about his problems later.* **PAT**: *Suppose that you buy Fred's house. You will regret that you could have bought a better house for a better price.*				
Grey Assessment State: Compound **Grey Degree**: 4	1	2	3	4

Analysis: Pat Compounds his fallacious arguments with **Emotional** fear tactics, **Ad Hominem** accusations of family abuse, irrelevant information, and another fear of regret over another possible choice of a better house. This amount of Grey Behavior warrants a Degree 4.

Fallacy 7 Two Wrongs Make a Right

"A form of flawed argument is to argue that an action is acceptable simply because someone else acted in a similar way" (Cottrell, 2005, p. 120).

Example 7.1: Selling Assets

> The opposition party is wrong to condemn the leader of the council for selling off public assets at a low price to its own supporters. When the opposition had a majority in the council, they sold off cemeteries and houses below the commercial price, benefiting their own supporters. If they can do it, then the current council can do it too.

Analysis: This is an example of the fallacy **Two Wrongs Make a Right**. It is wrong for any party to sell public assets cheaply in order to secure political advantages for their party. Just because a previous party did so, this does not make it right for other parties to follow suit. It may appear hypocritical to cast blame on another party for behavior that one's own party has engaged in. However, it would still be in the public interest for an apparently hypocritical politician to expose current wrongdoing. Otherwise, even more public assets would be wasted (Cottrell, 2005, p. 120, Passage 7.25).

Example 7.2: Stealing at Work

> Mr. Malcolm's employers pay their stylists much lower wages and expect them to work much longer hours than owners of other salons. Mr. Malcolm supplemented his income by taking equipment and styling products from the workplace and selling these in his own area. He was justified in stealing from his employer because his employer was exploiting him.

Analysis: The employers may have been in the wrong in the way they treated their employees. However, stealing was not the appropriate response. It isn't either ethical or legal. The argument **Two Wrongs Make a Right** would not stand up in court (Cottrell, 2005, p. 120, Passage 7.26).

Example 7.3: Dialogues

In the following four separate dialogues Pat displays increasing degrees of Grey Behavior. Read each dialogue carefully and assess the degree of Grey Behavior. The analysis following each dialogue explains the rationale and assigns a degree of Grey Behavior. Degree 1 indicates Pat commits a fallacy, but shows a Quick Correction after getting feedback from Chris. Degree 2 indicates Pat accepts that the statements are faulty and is convinced of committing a fallacy. Degree 3 indicates Pat commits a fallacy and shows a Recurrence of the same fallacy a second time even after more feedback from Chris. Degree 4 indicates Pat commits Compound fallacies.

Example 7.3_Dialogue 1: Pat and Chris are talking about the number of people attending last night's rally in support of one of Pat's social causes.

PAT: *Yes, I lied to you about the number. But, isn't there anyone else who lies but me?*

CHRIS: *There may be a lot of people who lie everyday but it doesn't justify us to do it.*

PAT: *You're right. Excuse me.*

Grey Assessment State: Quick Correction **Grey Degree**: 1	1	2	3	4

Analysis: Pat admits lying, but defends that because other people lie, thus arguing **Two Wrongs Make a Right.** He makes a **Quick Correction** so this is a mild Grey Behavior Degree 1.

Example 7.3_Dialogue 2

PAT: *Yes, I lied to you about the number. But, isn't there anyone else who lies but me?*

CHRIS: *There may be a lot of people who lie every day but it doesn't justify us to do it.*

PAT: *When there are so many people who lie, it doesn't matter!*

CHRIS: *If it doesn't matter what we say, we'll get used to lying the long term.*

PAT: *OK. You're right. Excuse me.*

Grey Assessment State: Convinced **Grey Degree**: 2	1	2	3	4

Analysis: Pat tries again to justify lying by saying "When so many lie, it doesn't matter," This is another example of the fallacy **Two Wrongs Make a Right. Chris** offers a counterargument that rampant lying would lead to its acceptance in the long run, **Chris** is **Convinced**, suggesting this is grey behavior at the degree 2.

Example 7.3_Dialogue 3	
PAT: *Yes, I lied to you about the number. But, isn't there anyone else who lies but me?* **CHRIS**: *There may be a lot of people who lie everyday but it doesn't justify us to do it.* **PAT**: *So, when there are so many people who lie, it doesn't matter!* **CHRIS**: *If it didn't matter what we say, we'll be used to lying in the long term.* **PAT**: *I won't lie if no one else lies!*	
Grey Assessment **State**: Recurrence **Grey Degree**: 3	1 2 3 **4**

Analysis: Pat repeats the original argument, "I won't lie if no one else lies." This Grey Behavior is Degree 3 because it is a **Recurrence** of the fallacy **Two Wrongs Make a Right.**

Example 7.3_Dialogue 4	
PAT: *Yes, I lied to you about the number. But, isn't there anyone else who lies but me?* **CHRIS**: *There may be a lot of people who lie everyday but it doesn't justify us to do it.* **PAT**: *I won't lie if no one else lies!* **CHRIS**: *This is not rational. You shouldn't lie again if you want to stay as my friend.* **PAT**: *Do you mean that you can find a friend better than me?* **CHRIS**: *I mean I don't want to make friends with anyone who lies.* **PAT**: *You are a person who thinks that only you're right and others are wrong!*	
Grey Assessment **State**: Compound **Grey Degree**: 4	1 2 3 **4**

Analysis: Pat is twice making the fallacy **Two Wrongs Make a Right.** After **Chris** warns **Pat** that lying again will lead **Chris** to drop **Pat** as a friend, **Pat** commits the **Straw Man** fallacy by saying *Do you mean that you can find a friend better than me?* This misrepresents what **Chris** said. **Pat** shows further grey behavior with the **Ad Hominem** fallacy of a personal attack on Chris as a person who thinks "*that only you're right and others are wrong!*" This **Compounding** of fallacies is an example of a heavy degree of grey behavior, 4.

Fallacy 8 Red Herring

"The **Red Herring** fallacy is committed when a person tries to side-track an argument by going off on a tangent and bringing up a different issue. Thus, the argument is then directed toward a different conclusion. The **Red Herring** fallacy is named after a technique used in England to train foxhounds. A sack of red herrings is dragged across the path of the fox to distract the hounds from their prey. A well-trained hound learns not to allow distractions to divert its focus from the prey. Because the red herring issue is often presented as somewhat related to the initial one under discussion, the shift in the argument usually goes unnoticed. The original discussion may even be abandoned completely and the focus shifted to another topic without the audience realizing what is happening until it is too late. The use of the **Red Herring** fallacy occurs in political debates when candidates want to avoid answering a question or commenting on a controversial issue. For example, a politician who is asked about a nationalized health care plan may change the topic to the less controversial one of how important it is for all Americans to be healthy and receive good health care. In doing so, the politician avoids having to address the question of which approach to health insurance he or she supports" (Boss, 2017, p. 150).

Example 8.1

I don't see why you get so upset about my driving after I have a few drinks. It's not such a big deal. Look at all the accidents that are caused by people talking on their cell phones while driving.

Analysis: The speaker shifts the topic to accidents associated with use of cell phones, the **Red Herring**, thus deflecting attention from the issue of his drinking and driving (Boss, 2017, p. 151).

The **Red Herring** fallacy also occurs in discussions of ethical issues when a person changes the topic from what *should* be to what *is*.

Example 8.2

ANGELO: *I don't think Mike should have lied to Rosetta about what he was doing last night. It was wrong.*

BART: *Oh, I don't know about that. If I had been in his situation, I would probably have done the same thing.*

Analysis: Here, **Bart** has changed the topic from what someone else *should* have done to what he *would* have done. In doing so, he changes the issue from a moral one to a factual one (Boss, 2017, p. 151).

Example 8.3: Dialogues

In the following four separate dialogues Pat displays increasing degrees of Grey Behavior. Read each dialogue carefully and assess the degree of Grey Behavior. The analysis following each dialogue explains the rationale and assigns a degree of Grey Behavior. Degree 1 indicates Pat commits a fallacy, but shows a Quick Correction after getting feedback from Chris. Degree 2 indicates Pat accepts that the statements are faulty and is convinced of committing a fallacy. Degree 3 indicates Pat commits a fallacy and shows a Recurrence of the same fallacy a second time even after more feedback from Chris. Degree 4 indicates Pat commits Compound fallacies.

Example 8.3_Dialogue 1: Pat and Chris are casual friends at the university. When they meet in the morning, Chris asks about the prior evening.			
CHRIS: *You promised you'd phone. But!?* PAT: *Did you pass your exam?* CHRIS: *I said, why didn't you keep your promise?* PAT: *Sorry! I forgot it.*			
Grey Assessment **State**: Quick Correction **Grey Degree**: 1	1	2	3 4

Analysis: Chris hinted **Pat** was not punctual after promising to call. Pat committed the **Red Herring** fallacy by asking about Chris' exam. With Chris' more direct question, "why didn't you keep your promise?" Pat apologized and showed a Quick Correction, Grey Behavior Degree 1.

Example 8.3_Dialogue 2			
CHRIS: *You promised you'd phone. But!?* PAT: *Did you pass your exam?* CHRIS: *I said, why didn't you keep your promise?* PAT: *I'm concerned about your exam.* CHRIS: *We can talk about it later. But now I'm talking about your punctuality.* PAT: *Sorry! I forgot it.*			
Grey Assessment **State**: Convinced **Grey Degree**: 2	1	2	3 4

Analysis: Pat tries the **Red Herring** again, expressing concern about Pat's exam. With **Chris'** more clear statement about **Pat'**s punctuality, **Pat** apologizes and is **Convinced**, thus the Grey Behavior Degree 2.

Example 8.3_Dialogue 3

CHRIS: *You promised you'd phone. But!?*
PAT: *Did you pass your exam?*
CHRIS: *I said, why didn't you keep your promise?*
PAT: *I'm concerned about your exam.*
CHRIS: *We can talk about it later. But now I'm talking about your punctuality.*
PAT: *Your success is more important than my punctuality!*

Grey Assessment State: Recurrence **Grey Degree**: 3	

Analysis: This is a **Recurrence** of the **Red Herring** fallacy by adding a statement that Chris's success is more important than Pat's punctuality, but still not explaining the failure to keep the promise to call. Result: Grey Behavior Degree 3.

Example 8.3_Dialogue 4

CHRIS: *You promised you'd phone. But!?*
PAT: *Did you pass your exam?*
CHRIS: *I said, why didn't you keep your promise?*
PAT: *I'm concerned about your exam.*
CHRIS: *We can talk about it later. But now I'm talking about your punctuality.*
PAT: *What do you mean? I'm not punctual at all!*
CHRIS: *I was waiting a long time to hear from you and you didn't call me.*
PAT: *You should learn how to communicate effectively!*
CHRIS: *I tried to call you but you didn't answer.*
PAT: *I didn't promise to call! I only said I call you if I can! Don't you want to stay my friend?*

Grey Assessment State: Compound **Grey Degree**: 4	

Analysis: The dialogue digresses further from the **Red Herrings** with more grey behavior from **Pat**: an extreme claim about **Chris:** "Do you mean I'm not punctual at all!" and **Straw Man** and **Appeal to Emotion** fallacies: "Don't you want to stay my friend?" This is a **Compound** set of grey behaviors: 4.

Fallacy 9 Irrelevant Conclusion

"Arguments that commit the Irrelevant Conclusion fallacy all end with a conclusion that is not related in any necessary way to the premises" (Barbone, 2018, p. 172).

Example 9.1

You cannot convict my client of murder. We have proven that one of the arresting officers made prejudicial remarks, remarks scornful of my client. Look at the videotape, the audiotape, the man's own testimony. He is a full blown racist; you must not trust anything he says.

Based on the O.J. Simpson case,
from PhilosophicalSociety.com

Analysis: In the above passage, the speaker's reasons are about the arresting officers but his/her conclusion is about not convicting their client of murder. These reasons are not relevant to the conclusion.

Example 9.2

More people should travel by public transport, as this would improve traffic flows in the city. If there were tolls for using roads, people would use public transport. Polls indicate that most people want the traffic flow to be improved. This shows that people would be willing to support the introduction of tolls. Therefore, the council should introduce heavy tolls.

(Cottrell, 2005, p. 115, passage 7.17)

Analysis:

There is an unwarranted leap to the conclusion that, because a poll shows people want the traffic flow to be improved, they would also support tolls. We are not told whether the poll asked questions about tolls, so we do not know that a toll would be welcomed. The public might have preferred a different solution, such as bus shuttles or car-sharing

(Cottrell, 2005, p. 116).

Example 9.3: Dialogues

In the following four separate dialogues, Pat displays increasing degrees of Grey Behavior. Read each dialogue carefully and assess the degree of Grey Behavior. The analysis following each dialogue explains the rationale and assigns a degree of Grey Behavior. Degree 1 indicates Pat commits a fallacy, but shows a Quick Correction after getting feedback from Chris. Degree 2 indicates Pat accepts that the statements are faulty and is convinced of committing a fallacy. Degree 3 indicates Pat commits a fallacy and shows a Recurrence of the same fallacy a second time even after more feedback from Chris. Degree 4 indicates Pat commits Compound fallacies.

Example 9.3_Dialogue 1. At a lunch break in the cafeteria, Pat and Chis are discussing Pat's co-worker Katherine.	
PAT: *Katherine never trusts me. If my boss doesn't replace her with a good person, he is not honest!* **CHRIS**: *Your boss's honesty is not relevant to your relationship with your colleague. I suggest you build her trust through careful work on a project together.* **PAT**: *That is a good suggestion.*	
Grey Assessment **State**: Quick Correction **Grey Degree**: 1	1 2 3 4

Analysis: Pat first says Katherine doesn't trust him, but then comments on the boss's honesty, which has nothing to do with Katherine's trust. This is an example of the **Irrelevant Conclusion** fallacy: the conclusion by Pat is unrelated to the premise about the boss. The result is a mild degree of grey behavior, 1.

Example 9.3_Dialogue 2	
PAT: *Katherine never trusts me. If my boss doesn't replace her with a good person he is not honest!* **CHRIS**: *Your boss's honesty is not relevant to your relationship with your colleague. I suggest you build her trust through careful work on a project together.* **PAT**: *But she may not listen to me.* **CHRIS**: *You should show her indirectly how you can be a helpful colleague to her.* **PAT**: *OK. Thank you for your advice.*	
Grey Assessment **State**: Convinced **Grey Degree**: 2	1 2 3 4

Analysis: In this dialogue, after the first exchange, **Pat** is still not convinced that **Chris'** suggestion is relevant. **Chris** elaborates on the relevance of working helpfully. **Pat** sees the relevance of the premise to the conclusion, and is **Convinced,** grey degree 2.

Example 9.3_Dialogue 3
PAT: *Katherine never trusts me. If my boss doesn't replace her with a good person, he is not honest!* CHRIS: *Your boss's honesty is not relevant to your relationship with your colleague. I suggest you build her trust through careful work on a project together.* PAT: But she may not listen to me. CHRIS: You should show her indirectly how you can be a helpful colleague to her. PAT: If I do it she may think that I'm a liar!
Grey Assessment **State**: Recurrence **Grey Degree**: 3   1 2 3 **4**

Analysis: In this dialogue **Pat** repeats the conclusion that Katherine considers Pat to be a liar. Pat is repeating the fallacy of **Irrelevant Conclusion,** warranting a score of 3 on grey behaviors.

Example 9.3_Dialogue 4
PAT: *Katherine never trusts me. If my boss doesn't replace her with a good person, he is not honest!* CHRIS: *Your boss's honesty is not relevant to your relationship with your colleague. I suggest you build her trust through careful work on a project together.* PAT: But she may not listen to me. CHRIS: You should show her indirectly how you can be a helpful colleague to her. PAT: *If I do it, she may think that I've fallen in love with her.* CHRIS: *Your dialogue should be professional, not personal.* PAT: *She is like a witch and nobody can get around her!*
Grey Assessment **State**: Compound **Grey Degree**: 4   1 2 3 **4**

Analysis: After **Chis** offers two attempts to make the premises related to Pat's conclusion, **Pat** makes an **Ad Hominem** fallacy of attacking Katherine's character by comparing her to a witch. This is not related to her alleged lack of trust in Pat. This shows Compound fallacious thinking degree 4.

SELF-ASSESSMENT 2

Now that you have learned about five more logical fallacies, here are three quizzes to check your understanding.

Quiz 2.1

Here are examples of the fallacies of the last five fallacies. After each example, write the letter for the fallacy in the space provided.

Examples	Fallacies
1. Yes, I was driving without having a driving license but there are some other problems more important than this. For example, many other drivers don't worn masks. ____ 2. Yes, I've lied but sometimes others lie to me too. ____ 3. My brother is the best player in the world because nobody is better than him. ____ 4. You must not fire her because she is bringing her kids up on her own. ____ 5. The idea will never work. Of course, the mainstream media like it, but they are known for their liberal bias. ____	a) Begging the Question b) Appeal to Emotion c) Two Wrongs Make a Right d) Red Herring e) Irrelevant Conclusion

Quiz 2.2

Read the following dialogue in a press conference carefully, In the space after each fallacy, write the name of the fallacy. Then state what response you would make if you could speak to Pat.

President Pat holds a press conference.

REPORTER 1: Protests and unrest increased in your presidential period. What is your solution?

PAT: We managed to raise the economic growth rate to 8% and this is the most growth a president has ever achieved in this country's history. ____

REPORTER 1: You still have not answered my question.

PAT: I answered, but you have not understood what I mean. They have protested against the government who has achieved such a success. They are ungrateful! ____

REPORTER 2: Why did you pull out of the deal?

PAT: We pulled out of the deal because we should have done it before. ____

REPORTER 3: Why did you insult the reporter last week?

PAT: She first insulted me. ____ If you continue this conversation, this means that you agree with their opinions! ____

Quiz 2.3

Read the dialogue and indicate the state and degree of Grey Behavior.

Dialogue between Pat and Chris about Pat's press conference.
PAT: How was my press conference? CHRIS: *You committed five fallacies!* PAT: It is usual for presidents to answer like this. CHRIS: *Maybe, but if you want to be a rational person you have to give a good argument even when you are under pressure in a political position.* PAT: You said such opinions when I was a candidate. But I won the race and now I'm a President. This shows us that we can achieve our goals without relying on logic. CHRIS: *You did win the election by committing a lot of fallacies. If people develop their ability to identify bad arguments in the future then you will hardly win the race.* PAT: You never encourage me. I don't want to listen anymore!

Grey Assessment	1	2	3	4
State: .... Grey Degree:				

Answers on page 117.

3 Grey Behaviors after Induction Fallacies 10–17

In this chapter,

- We analyze 8 induction fallacies defined in books by leading authorities.
- We give two examples from everyday life.
- We present a set of four dialogues in which Pat states a fallacious argument, Chris provides feedback, and Pat replies with differing levels of grey behavior.
- After each of Pat's responses we give our analysis of what was the bad argument.

After Fallacy 13 and Fallacy 17, you will have opportunities to complete a SELF-ASSESSMENT to check your level of understanding of the fallacies and the method of assessing the level of grey behavior following the fallacy.

Fallacy 10 Hasty Generalization

This fallacy is best understood by reading some examples.

> Each of the following is a general proposition, or generalization:
> 1. Water always flows downhill. 2. Large breeds of dogs have shorter life spans than smaller ones. 3. People in France are not very friendly to tourists. 4. Italians are quick-tempered. 5. Stockbrokers drive BMWs. 6. Bill never gets anywhere on time. General propositions make a claim about a category of things (water, dogs, Italians, etc.), attributing some characteristic to all members of the category. General propositions are normally supported by observing a sample of particular cases. But we often draw conclusions too quickly, on the basis of insufficient evidence. This fallacy, known as **Hasty Generalization**
> (Kelley, 2014, pp. 118–119).

Example 10.1

The food in L.A. is lousy, judging from this meal.

Analysis: The statement is a **Hasty Generalization**, because one meal is not an adequate sample to judge the food in L.A.

Example 10.2

> One version of **Hasty Generalization** is known as the **Argument by Anecdote**. An anecdote is a story. When a speaker or writer tries to support a general claim by offering a story, he commits this fallacy. A story is just a single incident. It may carry psychological weight, but it has little logical force. Here is an example of an argument by anecdote:
> > *Did you read where John Travolta flew his plane into LAX and parked it on the tarmac—right out there in everyone's way? That's the trouble with these Hollywood actors. They don't care about anyone but themselves.* (Moore & Parker, 2017, p. 196)

The story about Travolta parking on the tarmac is an everyday example to provide a compelling anecdote, but it is a fallacy of **Hasty Generalization** to charge that Hollywood actors don't care about anyone but themselves.

Example 10.3: Dialogues

In the following four separate dialogues, Pat displays increasing degrees of Grey Behavior. Read each dialogue carefully and assess the degree of Grey Behavior. The analysis following each dialogue explains the rationale and assigns a degree of Grey Behavior. Degree 1 indicates Pat commits a fallacy, but shows a Quick Correction after getting feedback from Chris. Degree 2 indicates Pat accepts that the statements are faulty and is convinced of committing a fallacy. Degree 3 indicates Pat commits a fallacy and shows a Recurrence of the same fallacy a second time even after more feedback from Chris. Degree 4 indicates Pat commits Compound fallacies.

Example 10.3_Dialogue 1: Pat and Chris are long-time friends. They are talking about abusive men.				
PAT: *My father was an abuser, and so was my ex-boyfriend John. All men are mean.* **CHRIS**: *Are you generalizing based on only 2 people?* **PAT**: OK. I should use a bigger sample to generalize.				
Grey Assessment **State**: Quick Correction **Grey Degree**: 1	1	2	3	4

Analysis: Pat readily realizes a sample larger than 2 is necessary to generalize to "all men" and **Quickly Corrects** her position, so the behavior is only mildly grey, degree 1.

Example 10.3_Dialogue 2				
PAT: *My father was an abuser, and so was my ex-boyfriend John. All men are mean.* **CHRIS**: *Are you generalizing based on only 2 people?* **PAT**: *All men who were related to me were cruel. Isn't that enough to conclude?* **CHRIS**: *Yes, it is enough to conclude that all the two men who were related to you as father and boyfriend were cruel. But your sample is too few to generalize to all men.* **PAT**: *OK. I got it.*				
Grey Assessment **State**: Convinced **Grey Degree**: 2	1	2	3	4

Analysis: In this dialogue, **Chris** has to explain further that **Pat** can generalize to men related to her but not to men in general, **Pat** is now **Convinced**. Here the behavior is somewhat more Grey, Degree 2.

Example 10.3_Dialogue 3

PAT: *My father was an abuser, and so was my ex-boyfriend John. All men are mean.*
CHRIS: *Are you generalizing based on only 2 people?*
PAT: All men who were related to me were cruel. Isn't it enough to conclude?
CHRIS: *Yes it is enough to conclude that all the two men who were related to you as father and boyfriend were cruel. But your sample is too few to generalize to all men.*
PAT: But, after all, I don't have a good feeling about men.

Grey Assessment **State**: Recurrence **Grey Degree**: 3	

Analysis: Even after **Chris** further clarifies the limits of **Pat's** generalization about meanness in men, **Pat** states she doesn't have a good feeling about men, a **Recurrence** of **Hasty Generalization**. This is a display of Degree 3 of Grey Behavior.

Example 10.3_Dialogue 4

PAT: *My father was an abuser, and so was my ex-boyfriend John. All men are mean.*
CHRIS: *Are you generalizing based on only 2 people?*
PAT: All men who were related to me were cruel. Isn't it enough to conclude?
CHRIS: *Yes, it is enough to conclude that all the two men who were related to you as father and boyfriend were cruel. But your sample is too few to generalize to all men.*
PAT: Do you mean that my conclusion is wrong?
CHRIS: *No. I didn't say that. I mean, in order to generalize your conclusion you should take more samples. You shouldn't commit a hasty generalization.*
PAT: Can you prove my claim is wrong?
CHRIS: *It was your claim that "All men are mean". And it is up to you to tell me how you can conclude such a claim.*
PAT: *It shows that you cannot prove my claim is wrong, consequently it is right!*
CHRIS: *My brother and my father are not mean. That is enough to show that all men are not mean!*
PAT: *According to you, this is too few to generalize!!!*
CHRIS: *Your claim is "all men are mean." Rewording of this claim is "No man is someone who is not mean." Therefore, if I can find at least one man who is not mean, I can prove your claim is wrong. Thus, because my brother and my father are not mean, we can conclude that your claim is wrong.*

> **PAT**: *You say that you can prove your claim with only by two men as evidence, but I have to give a lot of evidence of my claim. You should learn how to argue with other people!*
>
> **CHRIS**: *As I just said, we should give enough evidence, not a lot. If we don't have enough evidence, we commit the fallacy of* **Hasty Generalization.**
>
> **PAT**: *OK! I have a question. Suppose that we are hiking in a jungle and we understand we have gotten lost and we have lost our sense of direction. Suddenly we face a tiger. We have to quickly run away. I make my decision to go to the right and start running. Do you wait to gather enough samples to conclude which direction is correct?*
>
> **CHRIS**: *Your analogy is weak! This is an exceptional case that we have to decide intuitively because we don't have enough time to analyze. But now, we are not in an emergency situation and we should conclude logically based on evidence.*
>
> **PAT**: *That shows you cannot argue well!*

Grey Assessment **State**: Compound **Grey Degree**: 4	1	2	3	4

Analysis: In this dialogue, first **Pat** makes a **Hasty Generalization** that "all men are mean" based on experience with her father and boyfriend. **Chris** tries to show that evidence is not enough. **Pat** uses a weak analogy, that is tiger, to show some situations require such a quick decision which does not allow gathering many bits of evidence. Finally, **Pat Compounds** fallacies with an **Ad Hominem** that **Chris** cannot argue well. The combination of fallacies is Grey Behavior Degree 4.

Fallacy 11 Accident or Hasty Application

"This fallacy consists in applying a generalization to a special case without regard to the circumstances that make the case an exception to the general rule. **Accident** is the fallacy of **Hasty Application**" (Kelley, 2014, p. 120).

Example 11.1

It is illegal to use a cell phone while driving; therefore, that police officer committed a crime when she used her cell while driving.

Analysis: The general statement that it is illegal to use a cell phone while driving does not automatically apply to the special circumstance mentioned, that is the police officer. It is easy to imagine situations when police business might best be conducted on a cell. In addition, police presumably have intensive training handling a car in challenging conditions (Moore & Parker, 2017, p. 199).

Example 11.2

Many of you would not disagree that it is wrong to cut people with knives, and this is supported by the law. However, surgeons use scalpels to cut people open every day, and that's both legal and, most of us would say, moral. In this case, it would be illogical to argue that surgery is wrong or should be illegal based on the statement that it's wrong to cut people with knives. Surgery is an obvious exception, and almost all of us know that.

(https://philosophyterms.com/accident-fallacy)

Example 11.3: Dialogues

In the following four separate dialogues, Pat displays increasing degrees of Grey Behavior. Read each dialogue carefully and assess the degree of Grey Behavior. The analysis following each dialogue explains the rationale and assigns a degree of Grey Behavior. Degree 1 indicates Pat commits a fallacy, but shows a Quick Correction after getting feedback from Chris. Degree 2 indicates Pat accepts that the statements are faulty and is convinced of committing a fallacy. Degree 3 indicates Pat commits a fallacy and shows a Recurrence of the same fallacy a second time even after more feedback from Chris. Degree 4 indicates Pat commits Compound fallacies.

Example 11.3_Dialogue 1: At a community meeting to discuss their city's development plan, two committee members Pat and Chris are talking about shopping in a nearby neighborhood.

PAT: *This city has a very high crime rate; therefore, it will be dangerous to shop in this neighborhood.*
CHRIS: *It would be hasty generalization to draw a conclusion about a city's overall crime rate from what you observed in one particular location, at least if the city is large. Likewise, it is a fallacy to infer from the city's overall high crime rate, considered in and of itself without regard to anything else, that a particular location in the city has a high crime rate.*
PAT: *OK. We should get more information in this neighborhood.*

Grey Assessment **State**: Quick Correction **Grey Degree**: 1	1	2	3	4

Analysis: Pat commits the **Accident** fallacy by assuming the high crime rate in the city applies to the neighborhood being discussed. This neighborhood may well be an exception. **Pat** quickly makes a correction, Degree 1.

Example 11.3_Dialogue 2

PAT: *This city has a very high crime rate; therefore, it will be dangerous to shop in this neighborhood.*
CHRIS: *It would be hasty generalization to draw a conclusion about a city's overall crime rate from what you observed in one particular location, at least if the city is large. Likewise, it is a fallacy to infer from the city's overall high crime rate, considered in and of itself without regard to anything else, that a particular location in the city has a high crime rate.*
PAT: *It is a risky shopping in the neighborhood.*
CHRIS: *We should get more evidence to conclude that.*
PAT: *You're right.*

Grey Assessment **State**: Convinced **Grey Degree**: 2	1	2	3	4

Analysis: Pat is **convinced** the statement of a high crime rate is an **Accident** fallacy after **Chris** points out we need more evidence to say it is risky shopping in this neighborhood. The risk to shop there may be an exception, and actually low.

Example 11.3_Dialogue 3	
PAT: *This city has a very high crime rate; therefore, it will be dangerous to shop in this neighborhood.* **CHRIS**: *It would be hasty generalization to draw a conclusion about a city's overall crime rate from what you observed in one particular location, at least if the city is large. Likewise, it is a fallacy to infer from the city's overall high crime rate, considered in and of itself without regard to anything else, that a particular location in the city has a high crime rate.* **PAT**: *High rate in crime shows that we should be careful wherever we go.* **CHRIS**: *We should get more evidence to conclude.* **PAT**: *Gathering more information cannot reduce crime rate in this city!*	
Grey Assessment **State**: Recurrence **Grey Degree**: 3	1 2 3 4

Analysis: Pat's statement that a high rate of crime shows a need to be careful is a repetition of the original statement of danger to shop in this neighborhood. It is a **Recurrence** of the **Accident** fallacy, a Degree 3 Grey Behavior.

Example 11.3_Dialogue 4	
PAT: *This city has a very high crime rate; therefore, it will be dangerous to shop in this neighborhood.* **CHRIS**: *It would be hasty generalization to draw a conclusion about a city's overall crime rate from what you observed in one particular location, at least if the city is large. Likewise, it is a fallacy to infer from the city's overall high crime rate, considered in and of itself without regard to anything else, that a particular location in the city has a high crime rate.* **PAT**: *Crime rate is a measure not a fallacy!* **CHRIS**: *I didn't say it. I talked about your argument. I mean that this neighborhood may be safe.* **PAT**: *Can you prove this neighborhood is safe?* **CHRIS**: *I have not enough evidence now but it is up to you to bring enough evidence and reasons to prove your claim.* **PAT**: *You cannot prove that the neighborhood is safe, therefore it is dangerous!* **CHRIS**: *You are appealing to ignorance and are committing the fallacy of* ***Misplacing the Burden of Proof.*** *That means your claim is true simply because I cannot prove it is false. This is a fallacy.* **PAT**: *You just said you are ignorant. Why do I discuss with you!*	
Grey Assessment **State**: Compound **Grey Degree**: 4	1 2 3 4

Analysis: Pat states the **Accident** fallacy, and **Chris** explains the faulty logic of applying the general city crime rate to this neighborhood. **Pat** misquotes **Chris** which leads to the fallacy of **Misplacing the Burden of Proof** on **Chris** to prove the neighborhood is safe or therefore it is dangerous. And then **Pat** voices the personal, **Ad Hominem** fallacy by saying **Chris** is ignorant. The **Compound** fallacies mean this is serious grey behavior, a Degree 4.

Fallacy 12 Weak Analogy

A **Weak Analogy** occurs when a person draws a comparison between two concepts, situations, or things to link them together in an argument, even though the connection between the two is not strong enough to make the case. For instance, let's say you try to argue that apples and oranges taste the same because they are both fruit and are similar in size. It doesn't matter if apples and oranges share a few similar characteristics, both types of fruit taste entirely different.

(https://study.com/academy/lesson/the-weak-analogy-fallacy-definition-examples.html).

Example 12.1

Guns are like hammers—they're both tools with metal parts that could be used to kill someone. And yet it would be ridiculous to restrict the purchase of hammers—so restrictions on purchasing guns are equally ridiculous.

Analysis: While guns and hammers do share certain features, these features (having metal parts, being tools, and being potentially useful for violence) are not the ones at stake in deciding whether to restrict guns. Rather, we restrict guns because they can easily be used to kill large numbers of people at a distance. This is a feature hammers do not share – it would be hard to kill a crowd with a hammer. Thus, this is a **Weak Analogy**, and so is the argument based on it (https://writingcenter.unc.edu).

Example 12.2

The federal government is just like a private household. If it doesn't balance its budget, it will go bankrupt.

Analysis: This is a **Weak Analogy** because the federal government has ways of avoiding bankruptcy indefinitely that are not available to a private household. These include being able to raise taxes, print more money, and stimulate economic growth and foreign investment (Moore & Parker, 2017, p. 201).

Example 12.3: Dialogues

In the following four separate dialogues, Pat displays increasing degrees of Grey Behavior. Read each dialogue carefully and assess the degree of Grey Behavior. The analysis following each dialogue explains the rationale and assigns a degree of Grey Behavior. Degree 1 indicates Pat commits a fallacy, but shows a Quick Correction after getting feedback from Chris. Degree 2 indicates Pat accepts that the statements are faulty and is convinced of committing a fallacy. Degree 3 indicates Pat commits a fallacy and shows a Recurrence of the same fallacy a second time even after more feedback from Chris. Degree 4 indicates Pat commits Compound fallacies.

Example 12.3_Dialogue 1: Pat and Chris work together in related departments at their company. They are talking about Pat's work tasks.			
CHRIS: *Pat, why didn't you finish your project?* **PAT**: Suppose that your rally car has run out of petrol. Can you get the finish line? **CHRIS**: *If you were in a car, and ran out of petrol, and there was no petrol station to fill up, then you couldn't get the finish line!* *This is a weak analogy. I'm talking about your project.* **PAT**: *OK. I mean we should have set a deadline to be achievable.*			
Grey Assessment **State**: Quick Correction **Grey Degree**: 1	1	2	3	4

Analysis: Pat compares a car in a rally running out of gas and thus not finishing the race, which is plausible, to the reason the project was not finished. This is a **Weak Analogy** because the real reason was an achievable deadline was not set. **Pat** makes a **Quick Correction**, grey behavior at Degree 1.

Example 12.3_Dialogue 2			
CHRIS: *Pat, why didn't you finish your project?* **PAT**: Suppose that your rally car has run out of petrol. Can you get the finish line? **CHRIS**: *If you were in a car, and ran out of petrol, and there was no petrol station to fill up, then you couldn't get the finish line!* *This is a weak analogy. I'm talking about your project.* **PAT**: *The rally car is relevant because I didn't have enough time to do it, so it is similar to running out of petrol.* **CHRIS**: *But, time management was a good solution.* **PAT**: *Yes. I should learn how to manage my time.*			
Grey Assessment **State**: Convinced **Grey Degree**: 2	1	2	3	4

Analysis: Here **Pat** defends the rally car situation by saying there was not enough time to do the project. Chris explains time management was needed and **Pat** is Convinced, degree 2.

Example 12.3_Dialogue 3
CHRIS: *Pat, why didn't you finish your project?* **PAT**: Suppose that your rally car has run out of petrol. Can you get to the finish line? **CHRIS**: *If you were in a car, and ran out of petrol, and there was no petrol station to fill up, then you couldn't get the finish line!* *This is a weak analogy. I'm talking about your project.* **PAT**: *The rally car is relevant because I didn't have enough time to do it, so it is similar to running out of petrol.* **CHRIS**: *But, time management was a good solution.* **PAT**: *I was similar to a runner who was tired and had no energy to continue!*
Grey Assessment **State**: Recurrence **Grey Degree**: 3   1 | 2 | 3 | 4

Analysis: Pat doubles down on the rally car analogy by saying time was relevant in both situations of the rally and project. **Pat** offers a comparison to a runner getting tired, another, second, **Weak Analogy**. This **Recurrence** of the same fallacy shows Degree 3 of Grey Behavior.

Example 12.3_Dialogue 4
CHRIS: *Pat, why didn't you finish your project?* **PAT**: Suppose that your rally car has run out of petrol. Can you get the finish line? **CHRIS**: *If you were in a car, and ran out of petrol, and there was no petrol station to fill up, then you couldn't get the finish line!* *This is a weak analogy. I'm talking about your project.* **PAT**: *My colleague, Alex, didn't finish his project on time.* **CHRIS**: *Two wrongs don't make a right. Alex's performance is irrelevant to your project. I treat him like you. Now we are talking about your performance.* **PAT**: Alex is your friend and you don't want to force him. **CHRIS**: *Pat, Don't you want to tell me about your project?* **PAT**: *If you continue to pressure on me, I won't collaborate with you.* **CHRIS**: *We are colleagues and each of us has some responsibilities. I ask you about your project because we have to finish our project and deliver it on time to attract our customer satisfaction.* **PAT**: *You are talking about customer satisfaction while my satisfaction is not important to you!*
Grey Assessment **State**: Compound **Grey Degree**: 4   1 | 2 | 3 | 4

Analysis: Pat states three **Compound** fallacies: **Weak Analogy** – car rally and project; **Two Wrongs Make a Right** – colleague didn't finish his project on time; **Red Herring** – Chris' supposed pressure will destroy the friendship. This is Degree 4, the greyest of fallacious reasoning.

Fallacy 13 Mistaken Appeal to Authority

Often we add strength to our arguments by referring to respected sources or authorities and explain their positions on the issues we're discussing. If, however, we try to get readers (listeners) to agree with us simply by impressing them with a famous name or by appealing to a supposed authority who really isn't much of an expert, we commit the fallacy of Appeal to Authority
(https://writingcenter.unc.edu//tips-and-tools//fallacies).

Example 13.1

My priest says that genetic engineering is not safe. Therefore, all experimentation in this field should be stopped.

Analysis: Unless your priest also happens to be an expert in genetic engineering, before accepting his argument as correct, you should ask him for reliable and authoritative evidence for his assertion (Boss, 2017, p. 154).

Example 13.2

We often find this fallacy in advertisements in which celebrities are used to promote products. For examples, Lady Gaga and Tony Bennett team up in a holiday ad for Barnes and Noble, while NBA All-Star player Blake Griffin appears in an ad for Kia cars, and Olympic swimmer Michael Phelps appears in ads for milk. In none of these cases are the celebrities authorities on these products, and yet people accept their word simply because they are experts in unrelated fields.

(Boss, 2017, p. 154).

Example 13.3: Dialogues

In the following four separate dialogues, Pat displays increasing degrees of Grey Behavior. Read each dialogue carefully and assess the degree of Grey Behavior. The analysis following each dialogue explains the rationale and assigns a degree of Grey Behavior. Degree 1 indicates Pat commits a fallacy, but shows a Quick Correction after getting feedback from Chris. Degree 2 indicates Pat accepts that the statements are faulty and is convinced of committing a fallacy. Degree 3 indicates Pat commits a fallacy and shows a Recurrence of the same fallacy a second time even after more feedback from Chris. Degree 4 indicates Pat commits Compound fallacies.

Example 13.3_Dialogue 1: Pat and Chris are talking about the president lying.

PAT: *"My father thinks the president lied. Therefore, the president lied."*
CHRIS: *The fact that it is your father who thinks the president lied does not affect the probability that he did—unless, of course, the subject is something your father have special knowledge about.*
PAT: *OK! I shouldn't have accepted my father's idea about that.*

Grey Assessment **State**: Quick Correction **Grey Degree**: 1	1	2	3	4

Analysis: This is most likely an example of **Mistaken Appeal to Authority** because we have no evidence **Pat**'s father is an expert on the topic. **Pat** makes a **Quick Correction** showing a low level 1 of Grey Behavior.

Example 13.3_Dialogue 2

PAT: *"My father thinks the president lied. Therefore, the president lied."*
CHRIS: *The fact that he is your father who thinks the president lied does not affect the probability that he did—unless, of course, the subject is something your father would have special knowledge about.*
PAT: *But my father is a doctor and he is smart.*
CHRIS: *Uniforms and distinguished titles such as doctor, professor, president, and lieutenant also serve to reinforce the mistaken perception that people who are experts in one field must be knowledgeable in others. This phenomenon is known as the halo effect.*
PAT: *Can you tell me more about Hallo Effect?*
CHRIS: *Yes of course! The halo effect is a type of cognitive bias in which our overall impression of a person influences how we feel and think about their character. Essentially, your overall impression of father ("He is nice!") impacts your evaluations of his specific traits ("He is also smart!").*
PAT: *I got it. Thank you!*

Grey Assessment **State**: Convinced **Grey Degree**: 2	1	2	3	4

Analysis: Pat shows a **Mistaken Appeal to Authority**, with no evidence of the relevance of the father's expertise to the president's lying. **Pat**'s father is a nice doctor, but that is not relevant to the topic. When **Chris** points out these qualities may only create a halo, **Pat** becomes **Convinced** of the fallacy of this reasoning. The degree of Grey Behavior is Degree 2.

Example 13.3_Dialogue 3				
PAT: *"My father thinks the president lied. Therefore, the president lied."* **CHRIS**: *The fact that he is your father who thinks the president lied does not affect the probability that he did—unless, of course, the subject is something your father would have special knowledge about.* **PAT**: *But my father is a doctor and he is smart.* **CHRIS**: *Uniforms and distinguished titles such as doctor, professor, president, and lieutenant also serve to reinforce the mistaken perception that people who are experts in one field must be knowledgeable in others. This phenomenon is known as the halo effect.* **PAT**: *A doctor knows more than us!*				
Grey Assessment **State**: Recurrence **Grey Degree**: 3	1	2	3	4

Analysis: Another vague **Mistaken Appeal to Authority** that a doctor knows more than we do, is not relevant to the argument and thus is a **Recurrence** of the initial fallacy, showing a higher level of Grey Behavior 3.

Example 13.3_Dialogue 4

PAT: *"My father thinks the president lied. Therefore, the president lied."*
CHRIS: *The fact that he is your father who thinks the president lied does not affect the probability that he did—unless, of course, the subject is something your father would have special knowledge about.*
PAT: *But my father is a doctor and he is smart.*
CHRIS: *Uniforms and distinguished titles such as doctor, professor, president, and lieutenant also serve to reinforce the mistaken perception that people who are experts in one field must be knowledgeable in others. This phenomenon is known as the halo effect.*
PAT: *Didn't you ask your professor in school when you had a question in your mind?*
CHRIS: *Yes, I did. But that was relevant to the topic he was teaching.*
PAT: *Can you prove the president didn't lie!*
CHRIS: *This is misplacing the burden of proof on me, which is a fallacy. That was your claim that "the president lied" and you should have given enough reason to prove it.*
PAT: *You cannot make a good argument. You only try to detect flaws in other's argument.*
CHRIS: *I use my knowledge of critical thinking to evaluate arguments. We are talking about a claim you presented.*
PAT: *You are selfish because you see only from your view. One of your training needs is to develop your communication skills!*

Grey Assessment State: Compound **Grey Degree**: 4	1	2	3	4

Analysis: Pat's fallacies get **Compounded** as this dialogue continues. **Mistaken Appeal to Authority; Weak Analogy** – Pat's question about Chris' behavior in school; **Misplacing the Burden of Proof** – asking Chris to prove the president didn't lie; **Personal Attack** –*"You only try to detect flaws in other's argument."*; **Red Herring** by diverting the dialogue to **Pat's** supposed training need in communication skills. All this accumulates to the highest level of Grey Behavior, 4.

SELF-ASSESSMENT 3

Now that you have learned about four more logical fallacies, here are three quizzes to check your understanding.

Quiz 3.1

Here are four examples of the fallacies discussed in the four previous sections. After each example, write the letter for the fallacy in the space provided.

Examples	Fallacies
(1) My history teacher thinks that the government should increase the interest rate. ____	a) Hasty Generalization
	b) Accident (Hasty Application)
(2) The more fuel a car has the further it can travel. Workers are like cars. The more rewards they receive the more they can accomplish. ____	c) Weak Analogy
	d) Mistaken Appeal to Authority
(3) Surgeons cut people with knives. Therefore surgeons are criminals. ____	
(4) I always eat a lot of sugar and I've never had any problem. Therefore, sugar has no negative health effects. ____	

Quiz 3.2

Read the following monologue carefully. In the space after each fallacy, write the name of the fallacy. Then state what response you would make if you could speak to Pat.

Monologue by Pat in marketing a soft drink called "X"!
What better companion and friend than X! ____ More and more people around the world are drinking X because, as you have read in social networks, the sales of X has increased in New York City. ____ People always like to experience something enjoyable. Enjoy the lively taste by drinking X! ____

Quiz 3.3

Read the dialogue and indicate the state and degree of Grey Behaviors.

Dialogue between Pat and Chris about Pat's monologue.				
PAT: How was my marketing speech? **CHRIS**: *Your speech was more rhetorical than logical.* **PAT**: But in order to sell products, we have been trained to arouse consumers' emotions. **CHRIS**: *It is good you acknowledge you're not using logic! I think you should learn how to use argument and rhetoric together so that you can arouse emotions while using logic. I have a good friend who can coach you how to achieve this goal.* **PAT**: *Excellent! I'm eager to learn. Let's go!*				
Grey Assessment **State: ... Grey Degree: ....**	1	2	3	4

Answers on page 117.

Fallacy 14 Mistaken Appeal to Popularity

"The fallacy of **popular appeal** occurs when we appeal to popular opinion to gain support for our conclusion. The most common form is the *Bandwagon Approach* in which a conclusion is assumed to be true simply because 'everyone' believes it or 'everyone' is doing it" (Boss, 2017, p. 146).

Sometimes speakers and writers try to justify a practice on the grounds that is traditional or is commonly practiced. **Mistaken Appeal to Common Practice**, **Mistaken Appeal to Tradition**, and **Mistaken Appeal to Popularity** are variants.

Example 14.1: Appeal to Tradition

This is the right way; it's the way it has always been done.

Analysis: If tradition by itself truly justified a practice, then human slavery, burning people at the stake, and any other extreme and deplorable behavior would have been justified if it happened to have been "traditional" (Moore & Parker, 2017, p. 203).

Example 14.2: Popularity

Appeal to Popularity may use polls to support a conclusion.

Mandatory testing of students is a good measure of how academically effective a school is. A poll found that 71 percent of parents of children in grades K–12 "… favor mandatory testing of students in public schools each year as a way to determine how well the school is doing."

Analysis: The fact that most parents agree with mandatory testing is insufficient on its own to support the conclusion that it is a good measure of how well schools are doing. Instead we need a controlled scientific study to determine the relationship between criterion such as student test scores and how well a school is doing. This argument also contains an ambiguous term *well*. In order to conduct a study, we first need an operational definition of *well* (e.g., graduation rate) to determine how a school is doing. If we simply use student test scores we are engaging in circular reasoning, also known as the fallacy of **Begging the Question** (Boss, 2017, p. 146). The latter is Fallacy 5 in this book.

Example 14.3

In the following four separate dialogues Pat displays increasing degrees of Grey Behavior. Read each dialogue carefully and assess the degree of Grey Behavior. The analysis following each dialogue explains the rationale and assigns a degree of Grey Behavior. Degree 1 indicates Pat commits a fallacy, but shows a Quick Correction after getting feedback from Chris. Degree 2 indicates Pat accepts that the statements are faulty and is convinced of committing a fallacy. Degree 3 indicates Pat commits a fallacy and shows a Recurrence of the same fallacy a second time even after more feedback from Chris. Degree 4 indicates Pat commits Compound fallacies.

Example 14.3_Dialogue 1: At a coffee break at the organization Pat and Chris are talking about taking home a few office supplies.
PAT: *Everyone at this company takes home a few office supplies for themselves, so you can do it as well.* CHRIS: *In this case, not everyone at this company is taking home a few office supplies and nothing justifies it.* PAT: *Ok. You're right.*
Grey Assessment State: Quick Correction **Grey Degree**: 1　　1 2 3 4

Assessment: **Pat** asserts "everyone" takes home office supplies, with no evidence. **Chris** says that is not true and nothing justifies it. **Pat** readily agrees and makes a **Quick Correction**, showing only small level of grey behavior, 1

Example 14.3_Dialogue 2
PAT: *Everyone at this company takes home a few office supplies for themselves, so you do it as well.* CHRIS: *In this case, taking home a few office supplies is not true and nothing justifies it.* PAT: *But it is important what the majority of people do.* CHRIS: *You argue that something must be okay, or correct or reasonable because it is a common behavior or because most people do it. This is a fallacy. I have a question. Does the owner of the company agree with this action?* PAT: *No! You're right, it is not true.*
Grey Assessment State: Convinced **Grey Degree**: 2　　1 2 3 4

Analysis: After Pat first states "everyone" steals, and then the "majority" do it. After **Chris** labels these statements fallacy, and asks if the owner agrees with the practice, **Pat** is **Convinced** and acknowledges the claim is not true. **Pat** has made two **Appeals to Popularity**, but changes position, thus displaying a mild degree of Grey Behavior, 2.

Example 14.3_Dialogue 3

PAT: *Everyone at this company takes home a few office supplies for themselves, so you do it as well.*
CHRIS: *In this case, taking home a few office supplies is not true and nothing justifies it.*
PAT: *But it is important what the majority of people do.*
CHRIS: *You argue that something must be okay, correct, or reasonable because it is a common behavior or because most people do it. This is a fallacy. I have a question. Does the owner of the company agree with this action?*
PAT: *No matter! Most everyone does it.*

Grey Assessment				
State: Recurrence **Grey Degree**: 3	1	2	3	4

Analysis: Pat shows a **Recurrence** of the fallacy of **Mistaken Appeal to Popularity** in repeating the extreme assertion that "everyone" does it.

Example 14.3_Dialogue 4

PAT: *Everyone at this company takes home a few office supplies for themselves, so you do it as well.*
CHRIS: *In this case, taking home a few office supplies is not true and nothing justifies it.*
PAT: *But it is important what the majority of people do.*
CHRIS: *You argue that something must be okay, correct, or reasonable because it is a common behavior or because most people do it. This is a fallacy. I have a question. Does the owner of the company agree with this action?*
PAT: *Why would I think that? Do you think the owner of the company would take our viewpoints into consideration when he is making decisions?*
CHRIS: *That is irrelevant to our discussion. We are talking about "taking home a few office supplies."*
PAT: *These few things are not important to a big company.*

CHRIS: *Regardless of the office supplies' value, they do not belong to us. They are only for spending at work not for our personal home.* **PAT**: *We are creating a lot of value for our company, so we have a right to take home anything we need!*	
Grey Assessment **State**: Compound **Grey Degree**: 4	1 2 3 4

Analysis: After Pat makes two fallacious **Mistaken Appeals to Popularity**, **Pat** offers up a **Red Herring** by asking if **Chris** thinks the owner would take employee's viewpoints into consideration. When **Chris** attempts to get the conversation back to topic, **Pat** brings up another irrelevant **Red Herring** topic that employees create a lot of value for the company. This combination of assertions is a **Compound** of different fallacies and shows a higher degree of Grey Behavior, level 4.

Fallacy 15 Fallacies Related to Cause and Effect

Also called in Latin: Post Hoc Ergo Propter Hoc (After this, then because of this.)

> A person assumes, without sufficient evidence, that one thing is the cause of another. This can occur when we assume that because one event preceded a second event, it was the cause of the second event. Superstitions are often based on this fallacy:
> *"I wore my red sweater to the exam last week and aced it. I guess the sweater brought me good luck."*
> The fact that the good test performance follows wearing a red sweater is not evidence wearing a red sweater causes the good test performance.
>
> (Boss, 2017, p. 155).

Example 15.1

> I left the lights on when I went to bed. Next morning I woke up with a headache. Therefore leaving the lights on caused the headache.

Analysis: The speaker has overlooked the possibility that leaving the lights on and waking up with a headache may both be the effects of a common cause, such as having gone to bed unusually tired or intoxicated (Moor & Parker, 2017, p. 208).

Example 15.2

> Children with long hair are better spellers than children with short hair. Therefore having long hair makes a child a better speller.

Analysis: This premise is perhaps absurd, but the conclusion does not follow in any case. Having long hair and being a good speller may both be caused by some other third, preceding cause, for example, special child rearing practices of the parents. *Correlation does not prove causation* (Moor & Parker, 2017, p. 209).

Example 15.3: Dialogues

In the following four separate dialogues, Pat displays increasing degrees of Grey Behavior. Read each dialogue carefully and assess the degree of Grey Behavior. The analysis following each dialogue explains the rationale and assigns a degree of Grey Behavior. Degree 1 indicates Pat commits a fallacy, but shows a Quick Correction after getting feedback from Chris. Degree 2 indicates Pat accepts that the statements are faulty and is convinced of committing a fallacy. Degree 3 indicates Pat commits a fallacy and shows a Recurrence of the same fallacy a second time even after more feedback from Chris. Degree 4 indicates Pat commits Compound fallacies.

Example 15.3_Dialogue 1: At a book club meeting, Pat and Chris are talking about relationship between throwing out a chain letter and an automobile accident.

PAT: *After Susan threw out the chain letter and did not pass it along, she was in an automobile accident. Therefore throwing out the chain letter caused her to get in an automobile accident.*

CHRIS: *You have overlooked the possibility that the sequential events were coincidental.*

PAT: *I had doubt about it. You're right.*

| Grey Assessment
State: Quick correction **Grey Degree**: 1 | 1 | 2 | 3 | 4 |

Analysis: The simple observation by **Chris** that **Pat** overlooked the possible coincidence of throwing out a chain letter and the accident led **Pat** to retract the initial **Cause and Effect** fallacy. The minor grey behavior is scored 1.

Example 15.3_Dialogue 2

PAT: *After Susan threw out the chain letter and did not pass it along, she was in an automobile accident. Therefore throwing out the chain letter caused her to get in an automobile accident.*

CHRIS: You have overlooked the possibility that the sequential events were coincidental.

PAT: But, maybe it is true.

CHRIS: *Maybe. But you should have given enough evidence to make a good argument.*

PAT: You're right. I don't have enough evidence.

| Grey Assessment
State: Convinced **Grey Degree**: 2 | 1 | 2 | 3 | 4 |

Analysis: After **Pat** commits the initial **Cause and Effect** fallacy, **Chris** warns of the faulty logic, but **Pat** persists in the argument. **Chris** then says Pat should have evidence, and now **Pat** accepts there wasn't enough evidence and is **Convinced**. The pattern of grey behavior is scored 2.

Example 15.3_Dialogue 3				
PAT: *After Susan threw out the chain letter and did not pass it along, she was in an automobile accident. Therefore throwing out the chain letter caused her to get in an automobile accident.* CHRIS: You have overlooked the possibility that the sequential events were coincidental. PAT: But, maybe it is true. CHRIS: *Maybe. But you should have given enough evidence to make a good argument.* PAT: I believe in chain letters and I never do the same as Susan.				
Grey Assessment **State:** Recurrence **Grey Degree:** 3	1	2	3	4

Analysis: Pat voices a **Cause and Effect** fallacy of not passing along the chain letter causing the accident, is not persuaded there may be an oversight of coincidence of the two events, and voices a **Recurrence** of the same fallacy even after **Chris** points out the need for evidence. This is dark grey behavior, level 3.

Example 15.3_Dialogue 4
PAT: *After Susan threw out the chain letter, she was in an automobile accident. Therefore throwing out the chain letter caused her to get in an automobile accident.* CHRIS: You have overlooked the possibility that the sequential events were coincidental. PAT: Can you prove that throwing out the chain letter didn't cause the accident? CHRIS: *That was not my claim. It's up to you to support your claim. You should have given enough evidence to make a good argument.* PAT: When you receive a chain letter you should send copies of letter to more people. Everyone knows that. CHRIS: *This is a superstition and magical thinking. A* belief that some objects or actions are lucky or unlucky, or that they cause events to happen, based on old ideas of magic.

PAT: Magic has been part of our life for thousands of years.

CHRIS: *Magic is not a scientific approach. We should analyze events critically based on enough evidence.*

PAT: *You are telling me not to think about anything! All people cannot do the same as scientists. We believe in what we actually see.*

CHRIS: *You don't have to be a scientist to make a good argument. It is easy to argue only based on enough evidence.*

PAT: *We don't have to get a lot of information whenever we want to think about something. We have solved our problems so far and we go on forever.*

Grey Assessment	1	2	3	4
State: Compound **Grey Degree**: 4				

Analysis: In this dialogue **Pat** commits five fallacies. First, a **Cause and Effect** fallacy of the effect of tossing out the chain letter. Second, **Misplacing the Burden of Proof,** "Can you prove that throwing out the chain letter didn't cause the accident?" Third, **Mistaken Appeals to Popularity** "everyone knows that" and "old ideas of magic." Fourth, **Straw Man** fallacy, *"You are telling me not to think about anything!"* And then a **Red Herring** about the difference in ways of thinking by scientists (that is, argument based on evidence) vs common practice of solving problems without the need for a lot of information. This is a **Compound** of fallacious thinking a very dark set of grey behavior, degree 4.

Fallacy 16 Slippery Slope

"According to the **Slippery Slope** fallacy, if we permit a certain action, then all actions of this type, even the most extreme ones, will soon be permissible. In other words, once we start down the slope there is no holding back" (Boss, 2017, p. 157).

"It is a pretty good metaphor for the kind of situation in which, once you take the first step in a certain direction, circumstances will pull you further in that direction whether you like it or not, and you may slide too far down the slope" (Kelley, 2014, p. 121).

Example 16.1

> You should never give in to your child. If you do, soon she will have you wrapped around her little finger. You need to stay in control.

In this argument, there is no credible evidence that giving in to our children's demands once in a while will lead to their dominating us (Boss, 2017, p. 151).

Example 16.2

> No, I don't think we should tip servers 20 percent. The next thing you know we will be tipping them 25 percent, then 30 percent, and then who knows what. We will be giving out our entire paycheck every time we eat out.

What we should say to this speaker is "Why couldn't we stop at 20 percent?" We could also just say, "Give me a break" (Moore & Parker, 2017, p. 211).

Example 16.3: Dialogues

In the following four separate dialogues, Pat displays increasing degrees of Grey Behavior. Read each dialogue carefully and assess the degree of Grey Behavior. The analysis following each dialogue explains the rationale and assigns a degree of Grey Behavior. Degree

1 indicates Pat commits a fallacy, but shows a Quick Correction after getting feedback from Chris. Degree 2 indicates Pat accepts that the statements are faulty and is convinced of committing a fallacy. Degree 3 indicates Pat commits a fallacy and shows a Recurrence of the same fallacy a second time even after more feedback from Chris. Degree 4 indicates Pat commits Compound fallacies.

Example 16.3_Dialogue 1: Pat is a candidate for a city commissioner position. Pat and Chris are talking about gun control.

PAT: If we enact any kind of gun control laws, the next thing you know, we won't be allowed to defend ourselves against terrorist attacks.
CHRIS: *But police and security forces are responsible to uphold peace and security.*
PAT: *OK. You're right. Also, enacting gun control laws reduce terrorists' accessibility to guns.*

Grey Assessment State: Quick correction **Grey Degree**: 1	1	2	3	4

Analysis: Pat voices a **Slippery Slope** fallacy in saying any kind of gun law will eventually mean we cannot defend ourselves. Chris counters with an assurance police can protect us. **Pat** realizes there are even other preventions of falling down the slope, which shows a slight amount of grey behavior, level 1.

Example 16.3_Dialogue 2

PAT: *If we enact any kind of gun control laws, the next thing you know, we won't be allowed to defend ourselves against terrorist attacks.*
CHRIS: *But police and security forces are responsible to uphold peace and security.*
PAT: *We should not depend only on the police.*
CHRIS: *Also, enacting gun control laws reduce terrorists' accessibility to guns.*
PAT: *OK.*

Grey Assessment State: Convinced **Grey Degree**: 2	1	2	3	4

Analysis: After the first **Slippery Slope** fallacy against any kind of gun control, **Pat** objects that we cannot depend only on the police. **Chris** offers the reassurance that gun laws reduce access to guns among terrorists. This **Convinces Pat**, but the dialogue still shows some grey behavior, level 2.

Example 16.3_Dialogue 3
PAT: *If we enact any kind of gun control laws, the next thing you know, we won't be allowed to defend ourselves against terrorist attacks.* **CHRIS**: *But police and security forces are responsible to uphold peace and security.* **PAT**: *And when that happens, terrorists will take over our country.* **CHRIS**: *You concentrate on terrorist to distract. Enacting gun control laws reduce terrorists' accessibility to guns and also police can install a security system.* **PAT**: *Therefore, gun control laws will cause us to lose our country to terrorists.*
Grey Assessment   **State**: Recurrence **Grey Degree**: 3   1   2   3   **4**

Analysis: After the first expression of a **Slippery Slope** fallacy that any gun control will prevent us from defending ourselves, **Pat** warns terrorists will take over the country, and again asserts that gun control laws will cause us to lose our country. This series of comments displays a **Recurrence** of fallacious arguments results in level 3 of grey behavior.

Example 16.3_Dialogue 4
PAT: *If we enact any kind of gun control laws, the next thing you know, we won't be allowed to defend ourselves against terrorist attacks.* **CHRIS**: *But police and security forces are responsible to uphold peace and security.* **PAT**: Everyone is responsible to his or her own security! **CHRIS**: *Enacting gun control laws reduce terrorists' accessibility to guns and also police can install a security system. And these measures can reduce probability of terrorism.* **PAT**: *A security system violates our privacy.* **CHRIS**: *I agree with you about privacy but we should demand to keep our privacy. Now we should return to the main claim you first said about gun control laws.* **PAT**: *After such a law is enacted we cannot carry guns while police and terrorists will have access to guns. Therefore they will be able to take over us.*

CHRIS: *I'm giving you feedback on your argument. You committed a slippery slope fallacy. It is also a scare tactic (Appeal to Emotion).*
PAT: *We should consider consequences of our decisions.*
CHRIS: *Yes. But you should analyze all the advantages and consequences of the decision not stress on a bad situation only.*
PAT: *You don't understand the key points. You need to learn risk management.*
CHRIS: *Risk management is based on systematic analysis and objective argument but what you said is only a subjective opinion. You don't analyze the system scientifically.*
PAT: *Do you think that they are scientists who enact gun control laws!*

Grey Assessment				
State: Compound **Grey Degree**: 4	1	2	3	4

Analysis: In this lengthy dialogue, **Pat** expresses several fallacious arguments. First the **Slippery Slope** fallacy that any gun control law will mean we cannot defend ourselves from terrorists. Then **Pat** commits the diversion of a **Red Herring** that a security system violates our privacy. Then the scare tactic of **Appealing to Emotion** by saying police and terrorists will take over us. Finally **Pat** voices the **Straw Man** argument that misrepresents **Chris's** description of risk management. Namely, **Pat** asks if **Chris** thinks scientists are the ones who enact gun laws. This **Compounding** of fallacies shows the greatest degree of grey behavior, 4.

Fallacy 17 Untestable Explanation

"When someone offers an explanation that could not be tested even in principle, he or she is said to commit the fallacy of **Untestable Explanation**" (Moore & Parker, 2017, p. 212).

Example 17.1

He has heart issues because of sins done in a previous life.

This explanation is untestable. There is no way to tell if someone is a previous-life sinner. In fact we cannot even identify people who have had previous lives. Plus, who is to say that someone's past life was in a human form? Perhaps some of us had previous lives as bugs and such. We do not know if bugs are capable of sin, but we do know that we cannot distinguish a bug that has sinned from one that has not (Moore & Parker, 2017).

Example 17.2

He lied because he's possessed by demons.

This could be the correct explanation of his lying, but there's no way to check on whether it's correct. You can check whether he's twitching and moaning, but this won't be evidence about whether a supernatural force is controlling his body. The claim that he's possessed can't be verified if it's true, and it can't be falsified if it's false. So, the claim is too odd to be relied upon for an explanation of his lying. Relying on the claim is an instance of fallacious reasoning (www.iep.utm.edu).

Example 17.3: Dialogues

In the following four separate dialogues, Pat displays increasing degrees of Grey Behavior. Read each dialogue carefully and assess the degree of Grey Behavior. The analysis following each dialogue explains the rationale and assigns a degree of Grey Behavior. Degree 1 indicates Pat commits a fallacy, but shows a Quick Correction after getting feedback from Chris. Degree 2 indicates Pat accepts that the statements are faulty and is convinced of committing a fallacy. Degree 3 indicates Pat commits a fallacy and shows a Recurrence of the same fallacy a second time even after more feedback from Chris. Degree 4 indicates Pat commits Compound fallacies.

Example 17.3_Dialogue 1: In a university class on sociology, Pat and Chris are talking about moral decay and crime rate.

PAT: *The crime rate has gone up because of general moral decay.*
CHRIS: *Your explanation is untestable because it is too vague.*
PAT: *OK. The phrase "moral decay" is vague. We will have to agree and pin that down.*

Grey Assessment State: Quick correction **Grey Degree**: 1	1	2	3	4

Analysis: **Pat**'s assertion that moral decay is the cause of higher crime rate is an example of an **Untestable Explanation**. **Pat** realizes that "general moral decay" is too vague to provide a test of its effect on crime rate. Pat **quickly corrects** his thinking, showing a small amount of grey behavior, 1.

Example 17.3_Dialogue 2

PAT: *The crime rate has gone up because of general moral decay.*
CHRIS: *Your explanation is untestable because it is too vague.*
PAT: *How do you mean?*
CHRIS: *Moral decay, whatever it is, is not identical to a rising crime rate. Rather, the problem here is vagueness. We do not know what moral decay is exactly, and so we do not know how to test the assertion.*
PAT: *OK. I mean …*

Grey Assessment State: Convinced **Grey Degree**: 2	1	2	3	4

Analysis: In this dialogue **Pat** expresses the **Untestable Explanation**, and even questions what **Chris** means by the need for explanation of vagueness. This shows more grey behavior and thus it is grey degree 2.

Example 17.3_Dialogue 3

PAT: *The crime rate has gone up because of general moral decay.*
CHRIS: Your explanation is untestable because it is too vague.
PAT: How do you mean?
CHRIS: Moral decay, whatever it is, is not identical to a rising crime rate. Rather, the problem here is vagueness. We do not know what moral decay is exactly, and so we do not know how to test the assertion.
PAT: Our culture is losing its moral and ethical roots, so behaviors and principles of the society become rotten, therefore the crime rate goes up.

Grey Assessment State: Recurrence **Grey Degree**: 3	1	2	3	4

Analysis: In this dialogue **Pat** expresses the original **Untestable Explanation**, questions what **Chris** means about being too vague, and then does not address **Chris'** explanations. Rather **Pat** states a more elaborate version of the claim that our culture is losing its moral roots which leads to rising crime rate, thereby showing a **Recurrence** of the same fallacy. More grey behavior, degree 3.

Example 17.3_Dialogue 4			
PAT: *The crime rate has gone up because of general moral decay.* CHRIS: Your explanation is untestable because it is too vague. PAT: What do you mean? CHRIS: Moral decay, whatever it is, is not identical to a rising crime rate. Rather, the problem here is vagueness. We do not know what moral decay is exactly, and so we do not know how to test the assertion. PAT: Morality is beliefs about what is right and wrong and about how people should behave. And moral decay means moral corruption. It is easy to understand. CHRIS: I know what morality is. I mean we cannot measure exactly what moral decay is. Can you show me how to test your explanation? PAT: Everyone knows it. I don't know how you cannot understand it! Can you tell me what the cause of increase in the crime rate is? CHRIS: If I want to do it I should first do some research to get enough evidence to make a good argument. PAT: So! You cannot prove what is the cause, therefore my conclusion is right until you can prove it is wrong!!!			
Grey Assessment **State**: Compound **Grey Degree**: 4	1	2	3	4

Analysis: This **Compound** sequence of grey behavior includes: **Untestable Explanation** (the vague term "moral decay"), **Red Herring** (diversion to a definition of morality), **Mistaken Appeal to Popularity** ("Everyone knows it."), and **Misplacing the Burden of Proof** ("You cannot prove what is the cause, therefore my conclusion is right"). This full set of fallacies warrants a grey degree of 4.

SELF-ASSESSMENT 4

Now that you have learned about four more logical fallacies, here are three quizzes to check your understanding.

Quiz 4.1

Here are examples of the previous four fallacies. After each example, write the letter for the fallacy in the space provided.

Examples	Fallacies
(1) Every year the weather goes cold after schools are opened. Therefore, opening schools is the cause of lower temperatures. ____	a) Mistaken Appeal to Popularity
(2) I failed the exam because of bad luck. ____	b) Fallacies Related to Cause and Effect
(3) If you give him an inch, he'll take a mile. ____	c) Slippery Slope
(4) Everyone knows that Peter killed his colleague. Therefore, police should catch him. ____	d) Untestable Explanation

Quiz 4.2

Read the following report carefully. In the space after each fallacy, write the name of the fallacy. Then state what response you would make if you could speak to Pat.

Pat is speaking as a Sports News Expert!
The team has been eliminated from this year's edition of the Champions League after going down 0–1 to the rival. Everyone knows ____ that they were defeated after Peter left the team. ____ If it continues, the team will lose all their stars. ____ Only a new coach could break the spell. ____

Quiz 4.3_Dialogue between Pat and Chris about Pat's report.
PAT: How was my sports report? CHRIS: *Your arguments were not strong. There were four fallacies in your report.* PAT: Give me some good advice. CHRIS: *That was a pessimistic view based on only one defeat. You can interview their managers, players, and experts to get more information about the team. Then you can conclude where the team is.* PAT: That was a good suggestion. Thank you.
Grey Assessment **State:** … **Grey Degree:** ….   1 2 3 4

Answers on page 117.

4 Grey Behaviors after Formal Fallacies and Fallacies of Language 18–20

In this chapter,

- We analyze three fallacies defined in books by leading authorities.
- We give two examples from everyday life.
- We present a set of four dialogues in which Pat states a fallacious argument, Chris provides feedback, and Pat replies with differing levels of grey behavior.
- After each of Pat's responses, we give our analysis of what was the bad argument.

After Fallacy 20, you will have opportunities to complete a SELF-ASSESSMENT to check your level of understanding of the fallacies and the method of assessing the level of grey behavior following the fallacy.

Fallacy 18 Formal Fallacies

In a **Formal Fallacy**, the form of the argument itself is invalid. For example, the following argument contains a formal fallacy: "Some high school dropouts are men. No doctors are high school dropouts. Therefore, no doctors are men." Although the premises are true, the conclusion does not follow because the form of the argument is faulty (Boss, 2017, p. 137).

This fallacy results from a failure of form – which refers to the way the argument is set up. According to Moore and Parker (2017), three formal fallacies are:

1 Affirming the consequent
2 Denying the antecedent
3 Undistributed middle

Examples 18.1

In the following table, there are three kinds of formal fallacy, a description for each fallacy in the second column, an example for each fallacy in the third column, and an example of valid form for each fallacy in the fourth column.

	Formal Fallacy	Description	Example of Formal Fallacy (Invalid)	Example of Valid Form
1	Affirming the consequent: **If P then Q.** Q. **Therefore**, P.	"P" and "Q" stand for independent clauses – parts of claims that are true or false. (The part of the first premise after the "if" is the antecedent of the claim; the part after the "then" is the consequent.) Whatever clauses the two letters might stand for, if they are arranged according to the form in column 2, the result is an invalid argument.	**If** Jane is a member of a sorority, **then** Jane is female. Jane is female. **Therefore** Jane is a member of a sorority.	**If** Jane is a member of a sorority, **then** Jane is female. Jane is a member of a sorority **Therefore** Jane is female.

| 2 | Denying the antecedent:
If P then Q.
Not-P.
Therefore,
not-Q. | Just as we get an invalid argument, when one premise affirms the consequent of the other, the same thing happens when one premise denies the antecedent of the other (the antecedent is the part after the "if"). | **If** Sandy passed the final, **then** she passed the course.
Sandy did not pass the final.
Therefore, Sandy did not pass the course. | **If** Sandy passed the final, **then** she passed the course.
Sandy did not pass the course.
Therefore, Sandy did not pass the final. |
| 3 | Undistributed[a] middle fallacy
All M are P.
All S are M.
Therefore, all S are P. | This fallacy happens when a speaker or writer assumes that two things related to a third thing (the "middle") are otherwise related to each other. | All tigers are animals.
Some animals are poisonous.
Therefore, some tigers are poisonous. | All tigers are animals.
No animal is poisonous.
Therefore, no tiger is poisonous. |

a A distributed term is a term of the categorical syllogisms that is used with reference to every member of a class. If a term is not being used to refer to each and every member of the class, it is said to be undistributed (Kelley, 2014). To learn more about distribution see Chapter 7 in Kelley (2014) or Chapter 9 in Moore and Parker (2017).

Example 18.2: Dialogues

In the following four separate dialogues,

Pat displays increasing degrees of Grey Behavior. Read each dialogue carefully and assess the degree of Grey Behavior. The analysis following each dialogue explains the rationale and assigns a degree of Grey Behavior. Degree 1 indicates Pat commits a fallacy, but shows a Quick Correction after getting feedback from Chris. Degree 2 indicates Pat accepts that the statements are faulty and is convinced of committing a fallacy. Degree 3 indicates Pat commits a fallacy and shows a Recurrence of the same fallacy a second time even after more feedback from Chris. Degree 4 indicates Pat commits Compound fallacies.

Example 18.2_Dialogue 1: Pat and Chris are talking about dogs and their behavior.
PAT: *All German Shepherds are dogs. Some dogs bite. Therefore, some German Shepherds bite.* **CHRIS**: *Surprise! This conclusion does not follow.* **PAT**: *Yes. You're right. Both premises could be true and the conclusion false.*
Grey Assessment **State**: Quick Correction **Grey Degree**: 1   1 2 3 4

Analysis: Pat states two true premises (All German Shepherds are dogs. Some dogs bite), but the conclusion is false, because to say "some" dogs bite does not mean "all" dogs bite. German Shepherds may not bite. **Chris** correctly states that the conclusion does not follow. This is an example of the third form of **Formal Fallacies – Undistributed middle fallacy**. **Pat** agrees, thus showing a mild degree of grey behavior, 1.

Example 18.2_Dialogue 2
PAT: *All German Shepherds are dogs. Some dogs bite. Therefore, some German Shepherds bite.* **CHRIS**: *Surprise! This conclusion does not follow.* **PAT**: *Why?* **CHRIS**: *Both premises could be true and the conclusion false, as would be the case if, for example, all the biting German Shepherds (but not other types of biting dogs) suddenly died. If this happened, the remaining German Shepherds would all still be dogs, and it would still be true that some dogs bite, but it would not be true that some German Shepherds bite.* **PAT**: *OK*
Grey Assessment **State**: Convinced **Grey Degree**: 2   1 2 3 4

Analysis: Pat states two true premises (All German Shepherds are dogs. Some dogs bite.) but the conclusion is false, because to say "some" dogs bite does not mean "all" dogs bite. German Shepherds may not bite. This is an example of the third form of **Formal Fallacies – Undistributed middle fallacy**. **Pat** asks "Why" showing a reluctance to agree and says "OK" only after **Chris** explains in detail. **Pat** is **Convinced**, thus showing a bit higher degree of grey behavior, 2.

Example 18.2_Dialogue 3

PAT: *All German Shepherds are dogs. Some dogs bite. Therefore, some German Shepherds bite.*
CHRIS: *Surprise! This conclusion does not follow.*
PAT: *Why?*
CHRIS: *Both premises could be true and the conclusion false, as would be the case if, for example, all the biting German Shepherds (but not other types of biting dogs) suddenly died. If this happened, the remaining German Shepherds would all still be dogs, and it would still be true that some dogs bite, but it would not be true that some German Shepherds bite.*
PAT: *When you say that some dogs bite, and we know that all German Shepherds are dogs, therefore some German Shepherds bite.*

Grey Assessment	1	2	3	4
State: Recurrence **Grey Degree**: 3				

Analysis: Pat states two true premises (All German Shepherds are dogs. Some dogs bite.) but the conclusion is false, because to say "some" dogs bite does not mean "all" dogs bite. German Shepherds may not bite. This is an example of the third form of **Formal Fallacies – Undistributed middle fallacy. Pat** asks "Why" and **Chris** explains further that if all biting German Shepherds died, the remaining German Shepherds would be dogs and some dogs bite, but it would not be true that some German Shepherds bite. Despite this accurate logic, **Pat** repeats the **Formal Fallacy.** A **Recurrence** shows continued Grey Behavior and warrants degree 3.

Example 18.2_Dialogue 4

PAT: *All German Shepherds are dogs. Some dogs bite. Therefore, some German Shepherds bite.*
CHRIS: *Surprise! This conclusion does not follow.*
PAT: *Why?*
CHRIS: *Both premises could be true and the conclusion false, as would be the case if, for example, all the biting German Shepherds (but not other types of biting dogs) suddenly died. If this happened, the remaining German Shepherds would all still be dogs, and it would still be true that some dogs bite, but it would not be true that some German Shepherds bite.*
PAT: *If your premise, "all the biting German Shepherds (but not other types of biting dogs) suddenly died", don't you realize, my argument is true. Maybe they bear some biting dogs again!*
CHRIS: *Without considering my argument, your argument is an **Undistributed Middle Fallacy**. Maybe some biting dogs are all non-German Shepherds.*
PAT: *And maybe all of them are German Shepherds.*

CHRIS: *Yes. When we both use the word "maybe" shows we are not sure about it. Because of our uncertainty, we cannot draw the conclusion "some German Shepherds bite."*

PAT: You just want to prove "All German Shepherds don't bite". Do you have some personal reason for this conclusion?

Grey Assessment **State**: Compound **Grey Degree**: 4	1	2	3	4

Analysis: After the exchanges over **Formal Fallacies**, **Pat** impugns **Chris**'s motives by asking if **Chris** wants to prove "All German Shepherds don't bite" because of some implied malevolent advantage to be gained. **Pat** is making an **Ad Hominem (Personal Attack)** on **Chris**, which reflects **Compound**, dark Grey Behaviors, Degree 4.

Fallacy 19 Ambiguity

"Arguments that have ambiguous words or phrases, sloppy grammatical structure, or confusion between two closely related concepts can lead to **Fallacies of Ambiguity**. People with poor language and communication skills are more likely to use or fall for these fallacies" (Boss, 2017, p. 137).

Fallacies of ambiguity include **Equivocation** and **Amphiboly**.

- "**Equivocation** occurs when a key term in an argument is ambiguous—that is, when it has more than one meaning—and the meaning of the term changes during the course of the argument" (Boss, 2017, p. 137).
- "The fallacy of **Amphiboly** occurs when there is a grammatical mistake in an argument, which allows more than one conclusion to be drawn" (Boss, 2017, p. 138).

Example 19.1

All banks are alongside rivers, and the place where I keep my money is a bank. Therefore, the place where I keep my money is alongside a river.

Analysis: The fallacy in this example is called **Equivocation** or **Semantic Ambiguity**, and occurs when a sentence contains a word or phrase that is open to more than one interpretation (Moore & Parker, 2017, p. 224). In the example, the ambiguity comes because of the dual meaning of *bank*.

Example 19.2

If you want to take the motor out of the car, I'll sell it to you cheap.

Analysis: Just as **Equivocation** makes use of *semantic* ambiguity, the fallacy known as **Amphiboly** makes use of *syntactic* ambiguity. In these cases, it is the structure of the sentence that causes the ambiguity rather than a single word or phrase. In this example, the sentence's structure does not make it clear enough whether "it" refers to the motor or the car (Moore & Parker, 2017, p. 225).

Example 19.3: Dialogues

In the following four separate dialogues, Pat displays increasing degrees of Grey Behavior. Read each dialogue carefully and assess the degree of Grey Behavior. The analysis following each dialogue explains the rationale and assigns a degree of Grey Behavior. Degree 1 indicates Pat commits a fallacy, but shows a Quick Correction after getting feedback from Chris. Degree 2 indicates that Pat accepts the statements as faulty and is convinced of committing a fallacy. Degree 3 indicates Pat commits a fallacy and shows a Recurrence of the same fallacy a second time even after more feedback from Chris. Degree 4 indicates Pat commits Compound fallacies.

Example 19.3_Dialogue 1: Pat and Chris are talking about a claim dealing with the relative pay of workers and managers at a union meeting.

PAT: *They said that "workers make more money than managers do."*
CHRIS: *This is a special kind of semantic ambiguity with vague words: they, workers, and managers.*
PAT: *Yes. It contains ambiguous words.*

Grey Assessment State: Quick Correction **Grey Degree**: 1	1 2 3 4

Analysis: As **Chris** points out, in **Pat's** statement the words "they," "workers," and "managers" are examples of **Semantic Ambiguity**. Pat agrees, thus showing a slight grade of Grey Behavior, Degree 1.

Example 19.3_Dialogue 2 Pat and Chris are talking about a claim dealing with the relative pay of workers and managers.

PAT: *They said that "workers make more money than managers do."*
CHRIS: *This is a special kind of semantic ambiguity.*
PAT: *Could you analyze it?*
CHRIS: *This is true if the speaker refers to workers and managers collectively, since there are many more workers than there are managers. But it is obviously false if the two words refer to individual workers and managers.*
PAT: *OK.*

Grey Assessment State: Convinced **Grey Degree**: 2	1 2 3 4

Analysis: As **Chris** points out, in **Pat**'s statement the words "workers" and "managers" are examples of **Semantic Ambiguity**. When **Pat** asks for an explanation, **Chris** offers an analysis of when **Pat's** assertion is true (workers and managers collectively), but when it is false (individual workers and managers). **Pat** is **Convinced**, showing only a slight increase in Grey Behavior, Degree 2.

> **Example 19.3_Dialogue 3** Pat and Chris are talking about a claim dealing with the relative pay of workers and managers.
>
> PAT: *They said that "workers make more money than managers do."*
> CHRIS: *This is a special kind of semantic ambiguity.*
> PAT: *But it is clear that a worker makes less money than a manager.*
> CHRIS: *Maybe, but they should have said a more complete sentence so that there are no ambiguity to anyone. This is true if the speaker refers to workers and managers collectively, since there are many more workers than there are managers. But it is obviously false if the two words refer to individual workers and managers.*
> PAT: *But I think they know that.*
>
> | **Grey Assessment** | 1 | 2 | 3 | 4 |
> |---|---|---|---|---|
> | **State**: Recurrence **Grey Degree**: 3 | | | | |

Analysis: Chris insists that they should have said whether their statement referred to the collectives of workers and managers or to individuals so as to avoid ambiguity. **Pat** shows a **Recurrence** of **Ambiguity** by repeating the vague claim "they know that." This repetition deserves a Degree 3.

> **Example 19.3_Dialogue 4** Pat and Chris are talking about a claim dealing with the relative pay of workers and managers.
>
> PAT: *They said that "workers make more money than managers do."*
> CHRIS: *This is a special kind of semantic ambiguity.*
> PAT: *But it is clear that a worker makes less money than a manager.*
> CHRIS: *Maybe, but they should have said a sentence so that there would be no ambiguous meaning. This is true if the speaker refers to workers and managers collectively, since there are many more workers than there are managers. But it is obviously false if the two words refer to individual workers and managers.*
> PAT: *Their audiences were not kids!*
> CHRIS: *Claims or reasons should be clear to all.*
> PAT: *Have you never said ambiguous words or phrases?*
>
> | **Grey Assessment** | 1 | 2 | 3 | 4 |
> |---|---|---|---|---|
> | **State**: Compound **Grey Degree**: 4 | | | | |

Analysis: After **Chris** twice states the need for clarity of **Ambiguous** words, **Pat** voices an **Innuendo** (a rhetorical device) which would tell something unpleasant without saying it directly, namely not kids. **Chris** again insists claims and reasons should be clear … to all. **Pat** implies an irrelevant issue namely, whether **Chris** has ever said an ambiguity, thus **Compounding** the Grey Behaviors by implying **Two Wrongs Make a Right**. That combination is a dark degree of Grey Behavior, Degree 4.

Fallacy 20 Composition and Division

"The fallacy of **composition** consists in inferring that what is true of a part must be true of the whole" (Kelley, 2014, p. 123).

Example 20.1

The players of my favorite team are good players, therefore the team will win the cup.

Analysis: The fact that the members of a team are good players does not mean the whole team is good, because there are other factors such as communication among the members and tactics that make an effective team out of its members.

"The fallacy of **division** is the mirror image of composition: It is the inference that what is true of the whole must be true of the parts" (Kelley, 2014, p. 123).

Example 20.2

Men are taller than women.
Danny DeVito is a man.
Therefore, Danny DeVito is taller than the average woman.

Obviously, the concluding statement is incorrect, since the average woman – at 5 feet 4 inches tall – is 4 inches taller than Danny DeVito (Boss, 2017, p. 139).

Example 20.3: Dialogues

In the following four separate dialogues, Pat displays increasing degrees of Grey Behavior. Read each dialogue carefully and assess the degree of Grey Behavior. The analysis following each dialogue explains the rationale and assigns a degree of Grey Behavior. Degree 1 indicates Pat commits a fallacy, but shows a Quick Correction after getting feedback from Chris. Degree 2 indicates that Pat accepts the statements as faulty and is convinced of committing a fallacy. Degree 3 indicates Pat commits a fallacy and shows a Recurrence of the same fallacy a second time even after more feedback from Chris. Degree 4 indicates Pat commits Compound fallacies.

Example 20.3_Dialogue 1: Pat and Chris are good friends. They are talking about their investments.	
PAT: *During the recent recovery, my financial portfolio gained considerable value. Therefore, Microsoft stock, which is in my portfolio, gained considerable value.* **CHRIS**: *The fact that your portfolio as a whole increased in value during the recovery does not show that any particular investment within it increased in value during the recovery.* **PAT**: *Yes!*	
Grey Assessment **State**: Quick Correction **Grey Degree**: 1	

Analysis: Pat falsely states that because the portfolio gained in value, thus a part of the portfolio (Microsoft) gained in value. When **Chris** describes the fallacy of **Division**, **Pat** readily agrees, showing mild Grey Behavior, Degree 1.

Example 20.3_Dialogue 2
PAT: *During the recent recovery my financial portfolio gained considerably in value. Therefore, Microsoft stock, which is in my portfolio, gained considerably in value.* **CHRIS**: *The fact that your portfolio as a whole increased in value during the recovery does not show that any particular investment within it increased in value during the recovery.* **PAT**: *But the value of my portfolio is made up of its stock values.* **CHRIS**: *Suppose that your portfolio has two stocks S1 and S2 and P is the value of your portfolio (P = S1 + S2). If S1 goes up and S2 doesn't change, then P goes up. Therefore your portfolio gains in value while S2 does not.* **PAT**: *OK, I see.*
Grey Assessment **State**: Convinced **Grey Degree**: 2   1 2 3 4

Analysis: When **Chris** provides the clear example of the fallacy of **Division**, **Pat** agrees. Pat has shown a greyer Degree of Grey Behavior, Degree 2.

Example 20.3_Dialogue 3
PAT: *During the recent recovery, my financial portfolio gained considerably in value. Therefore, Microsoft stock, which is in my portfolio, gained considerably in value.* **CHRIS**: *The fact that your portfolio as a whole increased in value during the recovery does not show that any particular investment within it increased in value during the recovery.* **PAT**: *But the value of my portfolio is made up of its stock values.* **CHRIS**: *Suppose that your portfolio has two stocks S1 and S2, and P is the value of your portfolio (P = S1 + S2). If S1 goes up and S2 doesn't change, then P goes up. Therefore your portfolio gains in value while S2 does not.* **PAT**: *I think the portfolio is made of a collection of stocks in order to reduce the risk. The investors know how to make a good portfolio so that the value of it is made up of the parts.*
Grey Assessment **State**: Recurrence **Grey Degree**: 3   1 2 3 4

Analysis: Pat continues to ignore or misunderstand two explanations of the **Division** fallacy by **Chris**. Then **Pat** states the fallacy by using somewhat different words, simply showing a **Recurrence** of the first fallacious statement.

Example 20.3_Dialogue 4				
PAT: *During the recent recovery my financial portfolio gained considerably in value. Therefore, Microsoft stock, which is in my portfolio, gained considerably in value.* **CHRIS**: *The fact that your portfolio as a whole increased in value during the recovery does not show that any particular investment within it increased in value during the recovery.* **PAT**: *But the value of my portfolio is made up of its stock values.* **CHRIS**: *Suppose that your portfolio has two stocks, S1 and S2, and P is the value of your portfolio (P = S1 + S2). If S1 goes up and S2 doesn't change, then P goes up. Therefore your portfolio gains in value while S2 does not.* **PAT**: *I don't understand what you say. My mathematics is not good.* **CHRIS**: *So, suppose that a football team does its best and wins. Do you think that every member of that team has done his best?* **PAT**: *Yes. If one of the team members does not play well, the team cannot win. You cannot understand it. It would better to give an example: Suppose that your family is rich. Cannot we say that you are rich too?* **CHRIS**: *No. Maybe my parents and my brother are rich, but I have lost all my assets. And also, maybe they don't help me and I don't try to make more money. I'm not rich.* **PAT**: *But reality is different. Many rich people have inherited their wealth. You don't want to accept you're mistaken.*				
Grey Assessment **State**: Compound **Grey Degree**: 4	1	2	3	4

Analysis: This dialogue proceeds with **Pat** stating the **Composition and Division** fallacy and followed by **Chris**'s explanations. **Pat** then diverts the discussion by admitting a lack of understanding and poor math. **Chris** tries another example (that is, if a team does its best that means every member has done best). Pat says a family is rich that means each member is rich. **Pat** then diverts the dialogue with a **Red Herring** asserting that many rich people inherited their wealth. Finally, **Pat** committed **Ad Hominem** fallacy attacking **Chris**. Therefore, the degree of Pat's grey behavior is 4.

SELF-ASSESSMENT 5

Now that you have learned about three more logical fallacies, here are three quizzes to check your understanding.

Quiz 5.1

Here are three examples of the fallacies discussed in the three previous fallacies. After each example, write the letter for the fallacy in the space provided.

Examples	*Fallacies*
(1) We have done pretty well. Therefore we deserve appropriate rewards. ____ (2) The average of our team's scoring has increased over the season. That shows my performance has increased too. ____ (3) If students graduated from the university, then they have passed mathematics. She passed the mathematics course, therefore she graduated. ____	a) Formal Fallacies b) Ambiguity c) Composition and Division

Quiz 5.2

Read the following monologue carefully. In the space after each fallacy, write the name of the fallacy. Then state what response you would make if you could speak to Pat.

Monologue by Pat in the School Closure Campaign!
As you know, students are in quarantine in the coronavirus pandemic. Some people who are in quarantine don't do any work, therefore students should not do any homework. ____ They have to spend a lot of time in virtual space. They can't afford to pay the costs. Using the cellphone or computers makes their eyes weaken. ____ Distance learning is not a good choice for workshops or laboratories in a chemistry class therefore it isn't for all classes ____. We want to close schools or at least foreign students should return to their countries!

Quiz 5.3_Dialogue between Pat and Chris about Pat's monologue.

PAT: *How was my speech?*
CHRIS: *Your conclusion was unrelated to your reasons!*
PAT: *Can you prove what I have said are not true?*
CHRIS: *It is misplacing the burden of proof. Whoever has made a claim must give reasons. Your argument is strong if your reasons support your claims.*
PAT: *I expect you to encourage me but you always oppose me! You are not a good friend.*

Grey Assessment **State: ... Grey Degree: ....**	1	2	3	4

Answers on page 117.

5 Other Examples of Potentially Misleading Tactics That May Be Followed by Grey Behavior

In this chapter,

- We define rhetoric and describe several rhetorical devices.
- We define social influence techniques and describe several influence techniques.
- We define and describe attribution and cognitive errors.
- We distinguish among these three and how they differ from logical fallacies.

Rhetorical Devices

Rhetoric is the study of using words to persuade others in speech or writing (Blanchette & Richards, 2010; Corbett & Connors, 1998). Rhetoric is different from logical fallacy. It relies on the special choice of words which evoke emotions. The connotation of rhetoric can be neutral, positive, or negative. Historically, the word referred simply to a classical discipline, art, or science of persuasion. It involves the study of composition of cogent communication.

In a positive sense, rhetoric involves using words effectively. It is skill of speaking formally, being articulate, using reason to persuade others. Rhetoric is a skill of engaging in formal debate. An innocuous example is alliteration, that is, repeating the words in a phrase which have the same initial sound. For example, "Peter Piper picked a peck of pickled peppers."

Recently rhetoric has more often taken on negative connotations to criticize speech which is showy, artificially eloquent, and even manipulative or out-right lying. "Oh, don't believe that politician, he's just spouting a bunch of rhetoric."

We discuss rhetoric here because it can be used to divert attention from logical discussion of a substantive issue. Thus, we need to have a dialogue to explore the set of grey behaviors the speaker uses to understand the speaker's intent. It may be just the use of emotional appeal to gain our attention. Or the speaker may intend to mislead us. Effective leaders often use rhetorical appeals, sometimes for good or for evil. We cover rhetorical devices here to alert the reader that a speaker may be using rhetorical devices in a positive or negative way. You need to consider the context of the presentation, the general character and posture of the speaker, and his or her behaviors in a dialogue.

Variants of chosen words carry different emotional loadings. Here are some examples of how words or expressions have less or more emotion impact:

Detainee vs Prisoner
Very wealthy vs Obscenely rich
Eating meat vs Eating animal flesh
Elderly gentleman vs Old codger

A speaker who wants to put a positive spin on her message and arouse a more positive emotion will use the left-hand word; the speaker who wants to arouse a negative emotion will use the right-hand word.

Table 5.1 lists a few rhetorical devices. They all involve the use of words to arouse emotion. They play on the fact that words have more than literal or dictionary meaning.

To fully understand the speaker's intent when using a rhetorical technique, we need to consider the context of the speech and how the technique is used in combination with logical reasoning. You might judge the speaker less critically if he is using strong rhetoric

Table 5.1 Some Rhetorical Devices

Euphemism: emphasize agreeable aspects	Dysphemisms: emphasize disagreeable aspects
Weaslers: protect a claim by weakening it	Downplaying: tone down importance
Stereotypes: exaggerate a cultural aspect	Innuendo: use the power of suggestion
Loaded question: use a false assumption	Ridicule and sarcasm: put in bad light
Hyperbole: overdo an exaggeration	Analogy: idioms, figures of speech
Emotional analogies	Proof surrogates: do not name the authority being cited
Repetition: claim over and over	Demagoguery: fan fanaticism to propagate false ideas
Allusion: referring to something well known	Amplification: repeats a word for emphasis

and weak logic when trying to sell you his product, or if she is fan of her team in the stadium trying to encourage the players or arouse spectators. We expect rhetoric in those situations.

You might judge the speaker more harshly if he is using strong rhetoric and weak logic when he is the top manager in a company speaking to employees trying to motivate them to work harder without getting more rewards, or the speaker is arguing why a candidate is your best choice in an election. Here we expect sound logic and are wary of strong rhetoric.

Social Influence Tactics

Social influence refers to the ways people get others to change beliefs, attitudes, or behavior group (Branscombe & Baron, 2017; Myers & Twenge, 2019). Social influence tactics are different from logical fallacies. Whereas fallacies are errors in logic and thus literally not true, social influence tactics are factually true but they play on people's desire to conform to a group. These are everyday occurrences. They are effective because most people follow social norms, they are willing to conform, and want to be cohesive with a preferred group. These tactics can be used for good or evil; only the speaker's behavior in the context of the dialogue can determine which.

Table 5.2 lists some social influence techniques. Some rely on people's desire to be consistent over time; others rely on people's desire to reciprocate; still others are based on the fear of scarcity. A stronger influence technique is reliance on obedience, as demonstrated by studies showing people will comply with requests by authorities.

Attribution and Cognitive Errors

Attribution refers to the causes we give for our own behavior and the behavior of others (Aronson, Wilson, & Sommers, 2019;

Table 5.2 Some Influence Techniques

Appeal to social norms, conformity	Appeal to cohesiveness of group
Foot-in-the-door technique	Low-ball technique
Door-in-the face technique	That's-not-all technique
Obedience	Symbolic social influence

Graham & Folkes, 1990). In other words, attribution answers the question "To *what* do we attribute people's behavior?" In general, people's behavior is caused by personal (internal) characteristics or situational (external) circumstances or, of course, some combination. Describing my own job success, I might say "I did well on that job assignment because I worked hard and my boss helped a lot!"

In similar fashion, we often try to understand why other people do what they do in everyday life. That is, we assign causes for others' behavior. Whether these assumed causes for our own or others' behaviors are true depends on what we learn in the context of a fuller discussion with the speaker.

Attribution errors are tendencies to explain successful and unsuccessful behavior of ourselves and others in particular ways. These tendencies are errors when they lead us to false conclusions about the causes of behavior.

Table 5.3 shows a few attribution and cognitive errors. When explaining our own behavior, these errors arise because we try to protect our own self-image "The devil made me do it!" On the other hand, when explaining other people's actions we have a tendency to assume their actions are because of the kind of person they are "He gets in trouble just because he has a negative personality. He had it coming."

Attribution errors are different from logical fallacies. They are inferences we make about causes of behavior but not evidence related to the actual causes of behavior. Here's an example of the **actor–observer bias**: "You're clumsy; I slipped on the ice." The speaker attributes your accident to your clumsiness but his accident to a situational cause. "I'm good; you're lucky" illustrates the **self-serving bias**. In this tendency I attribute my own positive outcomes to internal causes but your success to an external cause.

People have a tendency to take credit for their successes by making internal attributions but to blame the situation (or others) for their failures by making external attributions.

Table 5.3 Attribution and Cognitive Errors

Optimistic and overconfidence bias	Magical thinking
Blaming the victim	Fundamental attribution error
Actor-observer effect (diminished responsibility)	Self-serving bias
Self-verification	Negativity bias

Table 5.4 Fundamental Attribution Error

Pat is interviewing for a promotion. Jan is another candidate.			
	Personal Characteristics		Circumstances
	Bad	Enabling	Interfering
Pat says "I attribute that: my *successes* to the fact	"I'm very talented and conscientious."		
my *failures* to the fact that			the economy was weak and my territory was bad."
Pat says "I attribute Jan's *successes* to the fact that:			"his family helped him and he had a good boss."
Jan's *failures* to the fact that		he is dishonest and lazy."	

Several attribution errors are summed up by the **Fundamental Attribute Bias**. See Table 5.4. In this example, two candidates, Pat and Jan, are being interviewed for promotion. In the interview Pat says

> I explain my successes by the fact that I'm very talented and conscientious. I explain my failures to the weak economy I faced and the bad territory I was assigned. Jan was successful because of help from his family. His failures were because he is basically dishonest and lazy.

Note that the speaker is attributing his own *success* to internal personal characteristics but *failures* to external circumstances. By contrast, when explaining Jan's behavior, Pat attributes Jan's *successes* to the circumstances of family help, but Jan's *failures* to his internal character flaws.

The only way we can ascertain whether these are accurate causes of behavior is through ensuing dialogues.

Table 5.5 Appeals of Different Misleading Tactics

Type of potentially misleading speech:	Appeal to:
Logical fallacies	Faulty reasoning
Rhetorical techniques	Emotions
Social influence tactics	Pressures to conform
Attribution and cognitive errors	Self-serving explanations

The Appeal of Different Misleading Tactics

Misleading tactics consist of logical fallacies, rhetorical techniques, social influence tactics, and attribution and cognitive Errors. You should watch for different attempts to influence or divert an argument from its core substance. Table 5.5 summarizes the different appeals to which different types of misleading tactics make.

6 Conclusions and Applications

In this chapter,

- We state several conclusions.
- We point out practical applications.
- We offer several applications for future research studies.

Conclusions

Now that you have read about 20 logical fallacies and other examples of misleading tactics, let's review what you have learned.

- You learned the definitions of logical fallacies from noted experts in the field.
- You learned to recognize examples of these fallacies in everyday situations.
- You learned how to assess the severity of fallacious thinking and grey behaviors by engaging in dialogues with the speaker.
- You know now not to judge too harshly someone who first commits a logical fallacy.
- Quizzes showed whether you have the skill to identify fallacies and assess fallacious thinking.
- You have read about rhetorical speech, social influence techniques, and errors in attributing the causes of behavior in yourself and others that can make situations where you need check the presence of grey behaviors.

In summary, this book has provided you tips on how to assess and avoid fallacious thinking and speaking that can sidetrack logical and effective arguments. You can apply these skills no matter what setting you find yourself.

**Grey Behaviors after Logical Fallacies
in Public and Professional Communication**
provides any reader a cognitive vaccination against being misled by
bad argument and grey behavior
in public and professional speech and writing.

Practical Applications

Here are a few examples of settings, where the book will help communicate effectively in public and professional settings.

Public Communication

- Journalists interviewing public figures
- Citizens participating in community meetings
- Family conversing in holiday gatherings
- Anyone engaging in civil discourse

Professional Audiences

- Interviewers screening applicants
- Managers at all levels conducting performance reviews and evaluating candidates for selection and promotion
- Assessors evaluating behavioral competencies in tests, situational judgment interviews, and assessment center simulations
- Sociologists interviewing members of groups, organizations, and societies
- Psychologists and other clinicians interviewing clients in behavioral assessment and development settings
- Teachers evaluating and developing communication skills in students
- Lawyers taking depositions in civil and criminal depositions
- Artificial intelligence engineers identifying and screening sensitive content, for example Twitter removes sensitive content such as violation, lies, and fallacies
- Authors of classical books on fallacies seeking a source to develop practical skills.

Grey Behaviors after Logical Fallacies in Public and Professional Communication can be used as a supplement to complement any book related to logic, reasoning, and fallacies. Table 6.1 shows a few examples.

Table 6.1 Books Related to Logic, Reasoning, and Fallacies

Arp, Barbone, and Bruce (2019)	Hurley (2008)
Bennet (2012)	Kelley (2014)
Boss (2017)	LaBossiere (2013)
Corbett and Connors (1998)	Lovell and Burke (2018)
Cottrell (2005)	Moore and Parker (2017)
Baggini (2018)	Paul and Elder (2012)
Epstein (2006)	Withey (2016)

Research Applications

The process of assessing grey behavior provides an operational method to study the correlates, use, and avoidance of fallacious thinking. Researchers can test subjects in experiments with samples of dialogues to obtain a "Fallacious Thinking Score." This score can be used as an independent variable and predictor in correlational studies and as a dependent variable to measure outcomes in experimental studies.

Industrial/organizational psychologists, human resource managers, and talent management consultants can use the method to supplement other methods to assess applicants to predict job performance and to train staff members. The method is especially useful when you are assessing and developing argumentative skills by AWD method (Kord & Thornton, 2020) or other similar methods.

Personality and social psychologists can use the behavioral assessment process to study the etiology of fallacious thinking in the biographical, early life, educational, and work experiences of people. Studies of personality characteristics using self-report questionnaires may vary with the extent of fallacious thinking.

Linguists can study the etiology and development of fallacious thinking in conjunction with other measures of personal variables such as demographic characteristics, cognitive abilities, values, and personality. They can also use the method as a pre- and post-measure to evaluate effectiveness of communication training programs. Through the judicious choice of fallacies, they can study which of the fallacies are more or less amenable to change.

Sociologists can study cultural differences in patterns of fallacious thinking. Initial application of the method described in the research report in the next passage suggest that applicants to that

Iranian company use Begging the Question, Hasty Generalization, and Irrelevant Conclusion most frequently, but Two Wrongs Make a Right, Untestable Explanation, and Composition and Division least frequently. Quite different patterns may emerge in companies in the US or Asian cultures.

Researchers will recognize the limitations of this method to assess fallacious thinking, as acknowledged throughout the book with the periodic warning signs and caveats.

Example of a Research Study

A large organization in Iran developed a method to assess applicants' argument skills in a recent recruitment process. The process included an assessment of grey behaviors along with argumentative and rhetorical skills in a new version of the behavioral assessment process, Analytical Writing and Discussion (Kord & Thornton, 2020). Out of 476 people who were assessed, 349 (73%) committed at least one fallacy. In total, 755 fallacies were committed. Table 6.2 shows the frequency of the 20 fallacies described in *Grey Behaviors*, listed from the most to the least frequent.

Figure 6.1 shows the Pareto Chart, Frequency of Fallacies. Figure 6.2 shows the percent of levels of severity of Grey Behavior shown in the dialogues.

Good News: nearly half (47%) of the speakers immediately self-corrected the fallacy after initial feedback and another 13% became convinced of the error after a bit more feedback in the dialogues.

On the other hand, 40% either repeated the fallacy or stated more fallacies as the dialogue continued.

Several practical applications of these statistics accrued to the organization. The assessment of grey behaviors contributed to the assessment of applicants for several staff positions as expert advisors to line managers. Experts in the organization had to have quite keen competencies to communicate complex information, engage in dialogues, and convince managers of the practical value of their expertise. The frequency of these fallacies gave the HR staff direction for building training methods. For example, the first six fallacies comprise 80% of the fallacies expressed by this group. This provided suggestions on how to train staff to be more effective in their communication, and thus avoid the common fallacies of Begging the Question and Hasty Generalization, and so forth.

Table 6.2 Frequency of Fallacies

Rank	Fallacy (Number)	Frequency of Fallacy	Probability of Fallacy Being Committed	Accumulated Probability[a]
1	Begging the Question (5)	127	0.36	0.36
2	Hasty Generalization (10)	98	0.28	0.56
3	Irrelevant Conclusion (9)	59	0.17	0.65
4	Appeal to Emotion (6)	52	0.15	0.72
5	Mistaken Appeal to Popularity (14)	50	0.14	0.76
6	Strawman (2)	49	0.14	0.80
7	Red Herring (8)	48	0.14	0.86
8	Ad Hominem (1)	44	0.13	0.89
9	Weak Analogy (12)	37	0.11	0.89
10	Slippery Slope (16)	33	0.09	0.92
11	Misplacing the Burden of Proof (4)	32	0.09	0.93
12	Ambiguity (9)	31	0.09	0.95
13	False Dilemma (3)	29	0.08	0.96
14	Mistaken Appeal to Authority (13)	16	0.05	0.97
15	Fallacies Related to Cause and Effect (15)	13	0.04	0.98
16	Accident (11)	12	0.03	0.99
17	Formal Fallacies (18)	11	0.03	0.99
18	Two Wrongs Make a Right (7)	8	0.02	0.99
19	Untestable Explanation (17)	4	0.01	0.99
20	Composition and Division (20)	2	0.01	0.99

a Accumulated probability is the union of successive fallacies. This probability follows the addition rule: $P(A \cup B) = P(A) + P(B) - P(A \cap B)$, where $A \cap B$ is the intersection of the two sets.

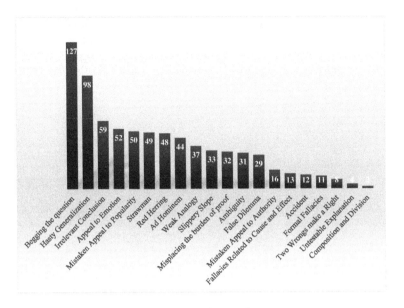

Figure 6.1 Pareto Chart, Frequency of Fallacies.

GREY ASSESSMENT

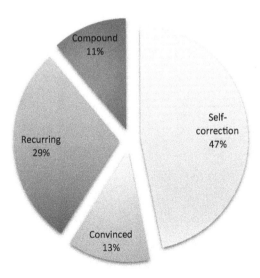

Figure 6.2 Percent of Levels of Severity of Grey Behavior.

The results also provided suggestions for additional research. Within the organization, the relationship of grey behaviors to argumentative and rhetorical competencies provides suggestions for combining the behavioral skills with other skills to improve the accuracy of assessment of individual candidates in recruiting.

References

Aristotle. (2015). *Rhetoric* (Translated by Rhys Roberts). Scotts Valley, CA: CreateSpace Independent Publishing Platform.

Aronson, E., Wilson, T.D., & Sommers, S.R. (2019). *Social psychology* (10th ed.). New York, NY: Pearson Education.

Arp, R., Barbone, S., & Bruce, M. (2019). *Bad arguments: 100 of the most important fallacies in western philosophy* (1st ed.). Hoboken, NJ: John Wiley & Sons.

Baggini, J. (2018). *How the world thinks: A global history of philosophy.* London, UK: Granta.

Barbone, S. (2018). Irrelevant conclusion. In R. Arp, S. Barbone, & M. Bruce (Eds.), *Bad arguments: 100 of the most important fallacies in western philosophy* (1st ed., p. 172). Hoboken, NJ: John Wiley & Sons Ltd.

Bennett, B. (2012). *Logically fallacious: The ultimate collection of over 300 logical fallacies.* Sudbury, MA: Archieboy Holdings.

Blanchette, I., & Richards, A. (2010). The influence of affect on higher level cognition: A review of research on interpretation, judgement, decision making and reasoning. *Cognition and Emotion, 24,* 561–595.

Boss, J.A. (2017). *THiNK: Critical thinking and logic skills for everyday life* (4th ed.). New York, NY: McGraw-Hill Education.

Branscombe, N.R., & Baron, R.A. (2017). *Social psychology* (14th ed.). London, UK: Pearson Education.

Corbett, E.P.J., & Connors, R.J. (1998). *Classical rhetoric for the modern student* (4th ed.). New York, NY: Oxford University Press.

Cottrell, S. (2005). *Critical thinking skills.* London, UK: Palgrave Macmillan Ltd.

Engel, S.M. (1994). *With good reason: An introduction to informal fallacies* (5th ed.). New York, NY: St. Martin's Press.

Epstein, R.L. (2006). *Critical thinking* (3rd ed.). Belmont, CA: Thomson Wadsworth.

Gambrill, E., & Gibbs, L. (2017). *Critical thinking for helping professionals.* New York, NY: Oxford University Press.

Graham, S., & Folkes, V. (Eds.). (1990). *Attribution theory: Applications to achievement, mental health, and interpersonal conflict.* Hillsdale, NJ: Erlbaum.

Hurley, P. (2008). *A concise introduction to logic* (10th ed.). Belmont, CA: Wadsworth Cengage Learning.

Kelley, D. (2014). *The art of reasoning: An introduction to logic and critical thinking.* New York, NY: Norton & Company.

Kord, H., & Thornton, G.C. III. (2020). Behavioral assessment of expert talent competencies: Analysis, decision making, and written and verbal communication skills. *Personnel Assessment and Decisions, 6,* 35–48.

LaBossiere, M.C. (2013). *76 fallacies.*

Lovell, S., & Burke, T. (2018). *Logical fallacies: Do you make these mistakes in reasoning?* Scotts Valley, CA: CreateSpace Independent Publishing Platform.

McCraw, B.W. (2018). Appeal to ignorance. In R. Arp, S. Barbone, & M. Bruce (Eds.), *Bad arguments: 100 of the most important fallacies in western philosophy* (1st ed., p. 106). Hoboken, NJ: John Wiley & Sons.

Moore, B.N., & Parker, R. (2017). *Critical thinking.* New York, NY: McGraw-Hill.

Myers, D.G., & Twenge, J.N. (2019). *Social psychology* (13th ed.). New York, NY: McGraw-Hill.

Paul, R., & Elder, L. (2012). *The thinker's guide to fallacies: The art of mental trickery and manipulation.* Lanham, MD: Rowman & Littlefield.

Paul, R., & Elder, L. (2014). *Critical thinking: Tools for taking charge of your professional and personal life.* Upper Saddle River, NJ: Pearson Education.

Russo, A. (2018). Burden of proof. In R. Arp, S. Barbone, & M. Bruce (Eds.), *Bad arguments: 100 of the most important fallacies in western philosophy* (1st ed., p. 136). Hoboken, NJ: John Wiley & Sons.

Thornton, G.C. III, Rupp, D.E., & Hoffman, B.J. (2015). *Assessment center perspectives for talent management strategies* (2nd ed.). New York, NY: Routledge.

Walton, D. (1998). *Ad hominem arguments.* Montgomery, AL: The University of Alabama Press.

Withey, M. (2016). *Mastering logical fallacies: The definitive guide to flawless rhetoric and bulletproof logic.* Berkeley, CA: Zephyros Press.

Appendix I

Answers to Quizzes in Self-Assessments

SELF-ASSESSMENT 1

Now that you have learned about the first four logical fallacies, complete the following quizzes to check your understanding.

Quiz 1.1

Here are examples of fallacies. After each example, write the letter for the fallacy in the space provided.

Examples	Fallacies
1 **Chris**: Does your job earn more money than before you got it? **Pat**: Do you mean that I have abused my position? __b__ 2 If you don't accept my claim, show me it's wrong. __d__ 3 If you want to be successful, you have to get a university degree. __c__ 4 You are supporting this proposal because you have interest in this project. __a__	a) Argumentum Ad Hominem b) Straw Man c) False Dilemma d) Misplacing the Burden of Proof

Quiz 1.2

The following monologue contains four fallacies. In the space after each fallacy, write the name of the fallacy. Then state what response you would make if you could speak to Pat.

Monologue. In a campaign speech for public office, candidate Pat says:

The ruling party has never done anything perfectly. They must be replaced now. __c__ They say it is difficult to reach an agreement with European Union this year. They mean we are not able to get any agreement. __b__

But I'm here to show that, in contrast with them, we are capable of doing anything. __a__ We can get the highest economic growth rate in the world and if they don't believe us, I tell them: can you prove we can't? __d__

Quiz 1.3

Read the dialogue and indicate the state and degree of Grey Behavior.

Dialogue between Pat and Chris about Pat's monologue.				
PAT: How was my speech? CHRIS: *You committed four fallacies!* PAT: You don't want me to win the race. CHRIS: *I would like you to win but not with bad arguments.* PAT: You are in the side of the ruling party.				
Grey Assessment **State**: ... Recurring... **Grey Degree**: ...3	1	2	3	4

SELF-ASSESSMENT 2

Now that you have learned about five more Logical Fallacies, here are three quizzes to check your understanding.

Quiz 2.1

Here are five examples of the previous five fallacies. After each example, write the letter for the fallacy in the space provided.

Examples	*Fallacies*
1 Yes, I was driving without having a driving license but there are some other problems more important than this. For example, many other drivers don't wear masks. __d__	a) Begging the Question b) Appeal to Emotion c) Two Wrongs Make a Right a) Red Herring b) Irrelevant Conclusion
2 Yes, I've lied but sometimes others lie to me too. __c__	
3 My brother is the best player in the world because nobody is better than him. __a__	
4 You must not fire her because she is bringing her kids up on her own. __b__	
5 The idea will never work. Of course, the mainstream media like it, but they are known for their liberal bias. __e__	

Quiz 2.2

Read the following dialogue in a press conference carefully. In the space after each fallacy, write the name of the fallacy. Then state what response you would make if you could speak to Pat.

President Pat holds a press conference!

REPORTER 1: Protests and unrest increased in your presidential period. What is your solution?

PAT: We managed to raise the economic growth rate to 8% and this is the most growth a president has ever achieved in this country's history. __d__

REPORTER 1: You still have not answered my question.

PAT: I answered, but you have not understood what I mean. They have protested against the government who has achieved such a success. They are ungrateful! _b_

REPORTER2: Why did you pull out of the deal?

PAT: We pulled out of the deal because we should have done it before. _a_

REPORTER3: Why did you insult the reporter last week?

PAT: She first insulted me. _c_ If you continue this conversation, this means that you agree with their opinions! _e_

Quiz 2.3

Read the dialogue and indicate the state and degree of Grey Behavior.

Dialogue between Pat and Chris about Pat's press conference.			
PAT: How was my press conference? CHRIS: *You committed five fallacies!* PAT: It's usual for presidents to answer like this. CHRIS: *Maybe, but if you want to be a rational person you have to give a good argument even when you are under pressure in a political position.* PAT: You had said such opinions when I was a candidate. But I won the race and now I'm a President. This shows us that we can achieve our goals without relying on logic. CHRIS: *You did win the election by committing a lot of fallacies. If people develop their ability to identify bad arguments in the future then you will hardly win the race.* PAT: You never encourage me. I don't want to listen anymore!			
Grey Assessment **State**: ... Compound... **Grey Degree**: ... 4....	1	2	3	4

SELF-ASSESSMENT 3

Quiz 3.1

Here are examples of the previous four fallacies. After each example, write the letter for the fallacy in the space provided.

Examples	Fallacies
(1) My history teacher thinks that the government should increase the interest rate. __d__	a) Hasty Generalization b) Accident c) Weak Analogy d) Mistaken Appeal to Authority
(2) The more fuel a car has the further it can travel. Workers are like cars. The more rewards they receive the more they can accomplish. __c__	
(3) Surgeons cut people with knives. Therefore surgeons are criminals. __b__	
(4) I always eat a lot of sugar and I've never had any problem. Therefore, sugar has no negative health effects. __a__	

Quiz 3.2

Read the following monologue carefully. In the space after each fallacy, write the name of the fallacy. Then state what response you would make if you could speak to Pat.

Monologue by Pat in marketing a soft drink called "X"!
What better companion and friend than X! __c__ More and more people around the world are drinking X because, as you have read in social networks, the sales of X has increased in New York City. __a__ People always like to experience something enjoyable. Enjoy the lively taste by drinking X! __b__

Quiz 3.3

Read the dialogue and indicate the state and degree of Grey Behaviors.

Dialogue between Pat and Chris about Pat's monologue.			
PAT: How was my marketing speech? CHRIS: *Your speech was more rhetorical than logical.* PAT: But in order to sell products, we have been trained to arouse consumers' emotions. CHRIS: *It is good you acknowledge you're not using logic! I think you should learn how to use argument and rhetoric together so that you can arouse emotions while using logic. I have a good friend who can coach you how to achieve this goal.* PAT: *Excellent! I'm eager to learn. Let's go!*			
Grey Assessment **State**: ... Convinced.... **Grey Degree**: ... 2....	1	2	3	4

SELF-ASSESSMENT 4

Now that you have learned about four more Logical Fallacies, here are three quizzes to check your understanding.

Quiz 4.1

Here are examples of the previous four fallacies. After each example, write the letter for the fallacy in the space provided.

Examples	Fallacies
(1) Every year the weather goes cold after schools are opened. Therefore, opening schools is the cause of lower temperatures. __b__	a) Mistaken Appeal to Popularity b) Fallacies Related to Cause and Effect c) Slippery Slope d) Untestable Explanation
(2) I failed the exam because of bad luck. __d__	
(3) If you give him an inch, he'll take a mile. __c__	
(4) Everyone knows that Peter killed his colleague. Therefore, police should catch him. __a__	

Self-assessment 4.2: Read the following report carefully. In the space after each fallacy, write the name of the fallacy. Then state what response you would make if you could speak to Pat.

Pat is speaking as a Sports News Expert!
The team has been eliminated from this year's edition of the Champions League after going down 0–1 to the rival. Everyone knows __a__ that they were defeated after Peter had left the team. __b__ If it continues, the team will lose all their stars. __c__ Only a new coach could break the spell. __d__

Self-assessment 4.3_Dialogue between Pat and Chris about Pat's report.
PAT: How was my sports report?
CHRIS: *Your arguments were not strong. There were four fallacies in your report.*
PAT: Give me some good advice.
CHRIS: *That was a pessimistic view based on only one defeat. You can interview their managers, players, and experts to get more information about the team. Then you can conclude where the team is.*
PAT: That was a good suggestion. Thank you.

| **Grey Assessment**
 State: ... Convinced...**Grey Degree**: ...2... | 1 | 2 | 3 | 4 |

SELF-ASSESSMENT 5

Now that you have learned about three more Logical Fallacies, here are three quizzes to check your understanding.

Quiz 5.1

Here are examples of the previous three fallacies. After each example, write the letter for the fallacy in the space provided.

Examples	Fallacies
(1) We have done pretty well. Therefore we deserve appropriate rewards. __b__	a) Formal Fallacies
	b) Ambiguity
	c) Composition and Division
(2) The average of our team's scoring has increased over the season. That shows my performance has increased too. __c__	
(3) If students graduated from the university, then they have passed mathematics. She passed the mathematics course, therefore she graduated. __a__	

Quiz 5.2

Read the following monologue carefully. In the space after each fallacy, write the name of the fallacy. Then state what response you would make if you could speak to Pat.

Monologue by Pat in the School Closure Campaign!
As you know, students are in quarantine in the coronavirus pandemic. Some people who are in quarantine don't do any work, therefore students should not do any homework. __a__ They have to spend a lot of time in virtual space. They can't afford to pay the costs. Using the cellphone or computers makes their eyes weaken. __b__ Distance learning is not a good choice for workshops or laboratories in a chemistry class therefore it isn't for all classes __c__. We want to close schools or at least foreign students should return to their countries!

Quiz 5.3_Dialogue between Pat and Chris about Pat's monologue.
PAT: How was my speech? **CHRIS:** *Your conclusion was unrelated to your reasons!* **PAT:** Can you prove what I have said are not true? **CHRIS:** *It is misplacing the burden of proof. Whoever has made a claim must give reasons. Your argument is strong if your reasons support your claims.* **PAT:** I expect you to encourage me but you always oppose me! You are not a good friend.

| **Grey Assessment**
State: ...Compound... **Grey Degree**: ... 4... | 1 2 3 4 |

Index